Heidi & Richard Adams
Saturday, May 9th,
Fredericksburg, Texas

Months before the wedding, the bride's planning board starts to fill up.

1:00 p.m. The bridesmaids' picnic, on the wedding day.

6:00 p.m. The reception tent is readied.

8.00 p.m. The ceremony begins.

Pioneer Museum,
Fredericksburg, Texas

May 9th, 8:00 p.m.

Semi-formal

260 guests

Candlelight service,
Holy Ghost
Lutheran Church

Vintage wedding
photographs, antique
bride and groom
cake topper

9:00 p.m. The celebration awaits the guests.

A WEDDING STRAIGHT FROM THE HEART

With the look of a family album from decades ago, the spring wedding of Heidi Wierdsma and Richard Adams captured the small-town heart of Fredericksburg, Texas. Setting up a tent at their local museum and drawing on the services of talented friends, the bride and groom created a wedding filled with community spirit and a reverence for the past. Invitations were presented on old postcards, the wedding cake was baked by a friend, and in the late hours of a starry Texas night, rose petals, sealed inside handmade wedding "crackers," joyously sent the bride and groom on their way.

romantic
weddings

Text by Mary Forsell

Foreword by Nancy Lindemeyer

HEARST BOOKS
NEW YORK

Library of Congress Cataloging-in-Publication Data

Victoria romantic weddings / by the editors of Victoria
        p.   cm.
  ISBN 0-688-15930-3
  1. Weddings—Planning. 2. Wedding etiquette. I. Victoria
magazine (New York, N.Y.)
HQ745.V52   1998
395.2'2—dc21   98-4091
                                  CIP

Printed in Italy

First Edition
10 9 8 7 6 5 4 3 2 1

www.williammorrow.com

EDITOR: Arlene Hamilton Stewart
DESIGNER: Gretchen Mergenthaler

PRODUCED BY SMALLWOOD & STEWART, INC.

table of

contents

Part Three This Fine Day

Foreword

"From this day forward" are words of promise. Weddings to me are wondrous because they are so filled with tomorrows. When guests gather, it is to reaffirm the power of love in all our lives.

Never have I been to a wedding that was not beautiful, nor seen a bride who was not glorious. I feel a bit like my grandmother saying that, because she always did. And when I was younger, sometimes I wasn't too sure she was right. But having been to many weddings now, I know it is true.

The other wisdom my grandmother imparted was that every bride should have the wedding she dreamed of. And dreams I have discovered are as individual as fingerprints. I have been to a simple home wedding where the bride mingled with guests until time for the ceremony. She was lovely in her mother's wedding dress, tailored for her. And I have been bewitched by a bride who walked a cathedral aisle as lovely as a princess. My own wedding was just the way I wanted it to be, an intimate gathering of family and friends.

In *Romantic Weddings* it has been our purpose to give brides-to-be ways to create that perfect, personal wedding. Every step of the day, from the first slip into a Cinderella slipper to the first dance as a married woman, is dedicated with affection and understanding to those who go "From this day forward" into lives where memories will be the jewels they truly cherish.

— NANCY LINDEMEYER, Editor in Chief

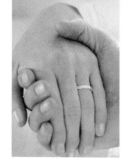

WHEN DREAMS BEGIN

For most brides, wedding dreams begin long before saying "I do." In your heart, you've always known what kind of bride you wanted to be — what you would wear, what kind of wedding you would have. Now, you've fallen in love and decided to marry. Suddenly, the time is at hand to plan a wedding and, just as brides have been doing for centuries, you begin moving toward the happiest of goals — making your own romantic wedding a reality.

Whether you elect a simple ceremony or a highly formal event, whether you're arrayed in a smart wedding suit or a cloud of white tulle, there are myriad decisions awaiting you as the bride. Wouldn't it be lovely to have a fairy godmother sweep down and make everything perfect? Of course, there are wedding consultants and other professionals, but even they

cannot make all the decisions. You know the

ring you want, the right balance of guests, and

how the invitation should look, the song to be played for your first dance.

But these are happy decisions ⁓ and part of the romance of modern-day

weddings. Never have the options been so liberating, giving you

the opportunity to personalize your wedding, to make it as

unabashedly romantic as you have always dreamed. Today's brides

are as well informed as they are adventurous, and they draw on

tradition and personal style to create a wedding that's a perfect

expression of their own joy and hope.

Savor these moments so that your

memories are as beautiful as your dreams.

THE FIRST STEPS

PERHAPS YOU ENVISION YOURSELF exchanging vows in a colonial farmhouse by candlelight, followed by an intimate meal with family and friends before the hearth. Or it may be that your passion is a grand cathedral with a vocal ensemble singing in the choir box and a reception at a riverside estate.

Above all else, the sites for ceremony and reception determine the wedding's mood and the extent of its guest list. Yet how does a couple sort through the possibilities? By all means, do not allow the usual conventions to limit you: There are many alternatives to the traditional route, and whichever you decide upon will be "right."

Let your mind drift through as many scenarios as possible: marriage at sea, on a city rooftop, in the chapel at your alma mater. Consider a romantic winter wedding at a rustic lodge, complete with skating parties. Bed-and-breakfast inns are especially suited to intimate weddings. Guests fill every alcove, and amidst the comfort of the surroundings, there is the tinkle of lively conversations and recountings of family lore.

Historic homes are wonderful wedding sites. For example, Hammersmith Farm in Newport, Rhode Island, features lush oceanfront gardens where through the years generations of brides and grooms have wed in grand style. Many of the National Trust for Historic Preservation properties accommodate large gatherings, which can be ideal if you imagine marrying in the hush of a richly panelled library and making a grand entrance into an elaborate Victorian ballroom with acoustics especially designed for a live orchestra.

The Restaurant Wedding

A stylish alternative to a traditional reception hall, the restaurant wedding is particularly appealing for more intimate parties with fewer guests. A favorite restaurant may be a more familiar environment for the wedding party, and that can contribute greatly to the festive atmosphere. With their professional staffs and reliable menus, restaurants are great work- and stress-savers. Many have private rooms that can be modified to order — with your own personal linens and silver serving pieces, and special lighting. Depending on the size and time of your gathering, the restaurant may design a menu just for you, and some will even print a commemorative menu card.

If you do decide on a restaurant wedding, make reservations for a dinner there shortly before your big day, to ensure every detail is just right.

a wedding far away

IF YOU'RE AN ADVENTUROUS BRIDE whose wedding fantasy has been marrying in a fairy-tale setting, then the "destination wedding" may be for you. The most romantic gesture possible, a destination wedding transports bride, groom, and guests to a far-off land for the ceremony and an extended party. This is truly a moveable feast, one in which the wedding celebration and honeymoon are rolled into one.

Thanks to the Internet, researching romantic places to marry has become an armchair adventure. In Europe, many châteaux and country estates welcome American wedding parties. For instance, the countryside in Britain is dotted with historic trust estates, many of which are listed in the travel books at your local bookstore.

As heavenly as a destination wedding may be, this is one time the services of a good travel agent and wedding coordinator are needed. Hire a coordinator based where you plan to marry, and investigate well beforehand the requirements for marrying in a foreign country (or even just another state in the U.S.).

THE HONOR OF YOUR COMPANY

WEDDING INVITATIONS ARE A PRELUDE to the event itself. An engraved invitation that is folded like a greeting card immediately indicates a formal affair. If the invitation is printed on colored stock ❧ perhaps with a swirl of botanicals or fleur-de-lys pattern ❧ and opens with a playful tug of a pretty silk bow, the recipient deduces an elegant wedding that will blend creativity with tradition. A vintage black and white postcard of a Sunday church picnic cleverly converted into a typeset invitation would promise an informal event infused with a strong family spirit.

The most formal invitations usually contain the following elements: a folded sheet of high quality stock such as pure cotton or linen, with a vellum overlay to protect the type, slipped into an unsealed envelope bearing the names of the guests. Also within are a self-addressed reply card and reception card, with travel directions. The entire package is contained by a fully addressed outer envelope. The most traditional invitations are engraved; lithography is not quite so formal but can have equally charming results when used with imagination. Calligraphy is another stylish option ❧ and one that you can personalize with different lettering styles and card stock.

If the guest list is under seventy-five, brides are free to hand-write their own invitations without any breach of etiquette.

Wedding programs, once the darlings of Victorian brides, are enjoying a revival. Handed out by ushers at the service, the wedding program, in addition to detailing the ceremony and the participants, could contain a special blessing or prayer for the bride and groom. After the wedding, programs become cherished keepsakes.

Friday - Rehersal Dinner

Saturday - Wedding

Sunday - Brunch

To ensure the privacy of this sacred occasion, it is im
wear the security pin provided. Your cooperation is

Interview

with a calligrapher
MARIA THOMAS

Hand-lettered wedding invitations are supremely elegant. Working from her studio in Whitinsville, Massachusetts, calligrapher Maria Thomas shares wisdom reaped from twenty years' experience:

"Wedding stationery lettered by hand only grows more beautiful with age. Calligraphy may be expensive, but couples can take lasting pleasure by framing and displaying their invitation at home after the wedding."

"Having every envelope calligraphed can become hugely expensive. Consider doing twenty-five addresses at the most, just for grandparents and other close family members."

"Calligraphers also design invitations to bridesmaids' lunches, menu and place cards for the wedding itself, the wedding program, and, most beautifully, a wedding certificate."

"Couples send out their wedding invitations six to eight weeks before the wedding, but most calligraphers need seven to twelve weeks before that mailing date to complete their work."

"Five of my often-requested lettering styles are: Chancery, the most classic look; Formal Italic; Spencerian, the ultra-swirly style dating from the 1890s; Roman, in which all the letters are the same size, resembling printing; and Celtos, which looks like Celtic lettering, but softer. You can combine styles — for instance, on a wedding program, the bride and groom's names in Spencerian lettering and all the other information in Chancery."

"Meeting with a calligrapher in person is always best; that way a bride can see actual samples of lettering on different kinds of card stocks, those with a smooth finish and others with a deckle, or rough, edge. The paper should always have a high natural fiber content, so that it will have longevity."

"Sometimes brides suggest calligraphy on a colored stock, which I think could be a mistake. Even the simplest of my calligraphy is so fancy in itself, why have colors compete with the artistry? For brides who want a splash of color, I suggest one of my soft watercolor rosebuds or another flower as a flourish. This kind of delicate touch might be

enhanced, perhaps entwining the monogram of the couple's married initials."

"When it comes to wedding programs, which contain a great deal of information, it's most cost-effective to have the cover calligraphed and the information inside typeset. In that way, the beauty of the calligraphy is prominent, and the ancillary information very easily read."

"The most personal of all wedding keepsakes is a calligraphed scroll, which each guest is asked to sign. I suggest that after the wedding, the couple take the scroll to a good framer."

OF ALL THE FESTIVITIES THAT HERALD a wedding, from the engagement party to the rehearsal dinner, none is closer to a bride's heart than the party she hosts in honor of her attendants — the maid or matron of honor, the bridesmaids, and the flower girl.

This is an opportunity for the bride to thank her attendants for all their devotion; it may take place at tea-time in late afternoon, or it can as easily be anything from brunch to a Champagne supper. The party takes place sometime in the week just before the wedding, and features lovely touches such as a layer cake containing silver charms in the shape of anchors, knots, hearts, thimbles, and horseshoes, representing marital happiness. Heartfelt toasts from the bride to her attendants are made in crystal stemware; hand-made favors send bridesmaids on their way.

Such an unabashedly feminine affair is a perfect stage for overtly feminine touches. Whether the celebration is in a summer garden or a library in winter, yards and yards of tulle should billow about the setting. As inexpensive as it is ethereal, tulle is virtually synonomous with brides and weddings. From canopies to table skirts to chandeliers, swags of tulle will imbue the party with the splendor of all things bridal.

Crisp tea linens, three-tiered silver caddies, Grandmother's china and candelabra, footed cake servers . . . all are in the tabletop repertoire. To set a festive mood, there must be an abundance of fresh fragrant flowers: tussie-mussies, pots of blooms, garlands draped from tables and chair-backs. The flowers planned for the wedding can be previewed here, or simple, casual arrangements of fresh-cut garden flowers can be featured.

In the past, bridesmaids played a less ceremonial, more active role in a wedding, making favors, gathering flowers, even decorating the bride's new home. This party helped the bride to repay their kindness, and it always concluded with a gift. Often, the gift was an exquisite pair of gloves or pearl earrings to be worn at the wedding.

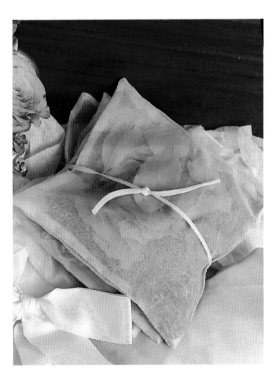

A Token of My Esteem

Certainly, gloves are still a sweet suggestion, but there are so many other classic choices. Delicate handkerchiefs, whether new or vintage, are sentimental tokens of esteem, with hand-embroidered initials or Renaissance lace edging. A bride might sew up silken sachets of potpourri and give them to attendants for lasting thanks. Jewelry remains a time-honored choice for attendants to both the bride and groom. If a bride wants each of her attendants to wear a matching locket or earrings, she would be wise to choose them as this gift. And grooms might give their attendants matching pearl studs and cuff links. Personalizing these gifts, either with embroidery or engraving, makes them that much more thoughtful and precious.

ONCE UPON A TIME, WHEN A BRIDE crossed the threshold of her new home, she came prepared with her trousseau — loosely translated as "bundle" in French — of all the household linens she would need for a lifetime, to be used again and again and then passed on to the next generation. This practical idea is experiencing a renaissance, as couples dress their homes in the highest quality trousseaux.

A bride usually assembles the trousseau herself. Department stores and catalogs offer good linens, but they are not always the most elegant ones available. In the quiet corners of understated linens boutiques, contemporary linens with all the charm of the past await: Italian damask tablecloths and napkins framed in handmade Venice lace, pillowcases trimmed with crochet work, embroidered bed canopies and coverlets, bed skirts with eyelet edges, handknit throws, and guest towels with charming decorative stitchery.

So, too, resourceful brides look to the linen closets of the past to stock theirs anew: Restored linens of all descriptions, from Victorian teacloths to 1930s linen tablecloths, can be had at auctions and antiques shops. Breathtaking in their design and their stitching, these wonderful linens should be scooped up, regardless of their monograms.

Art of the Monogram

In the past, every young girl learned to embroider linen at her mother's knee, so that by the time she became a married woman, each cloth in her trousseau would be graced with her monogram.

When you monogram linens they take on a personal air. Design yours with the help of a book of typography and a capable seamstress or a machine-stitching shop.

Interview

with a trousseau expert
ALENA GERLI

At her Pleasantville, New York, company, White Linen, Alena Gerli has witnessed the revival of the trousseau. Here she demonstrates her very European philosophy: buy less but opt for better quality.

"The Victorian bride's trousseau was twelve of everything: bed, bath, and dining linens. Nowadays, we look for the smaller trousseau so the bride is not overly committed to any one color or design."

"To start her trousseau, the bride should register with a linen specialty shop that carries high-quality bed, bath, and table linens. Though many of these shops are small, they offer many more choices than what is usually found in department stores or through catalogs. In addition to what they have on shelves, they will have fabric samples for you to take home."

"When selecting bed linens, choose only pure cotton of the highest possible quality within your budget. Look for at least a two hundred-thread count, but also a high-quality yarn such as Egyptian. A person can tell quality with the eye and hand: fabric must have a smooth sheen and feel soft to the touch. Of course, the very best, very finest bed linens are of linen, and if you can afford them, they will last for years."

"Select bedding colors and patterns that mix and match well: white, ecru, celadon, champagne.

Bold, bright patterns limit you. People no longer buy matching sets but coordinate color, texture, and pattern. For the master bedroom, a couple could start with two top and bottom sheets and several pillowcases. This may seem modest, but high-quality linens are costly. Add to your trousseau over time to build up a supply. "

"For special occasions, an embroidered tablecloth either in cutwork or drawnwork looks beautiful spread over a bare table."

"Most linens shops also offer monogramming. You select the stitching and decorative borders, and machines do the work. You can combine styles, and the monogram looks so wonderful, you'd never know it wasn't stitched by hand."

"For everyday dining, it's useful to have a damask cloth in one hundred percent linen or cotton and at least six placemats."

"One can never have too many cloth napkins. They instantly change the look of the table. Start with a dozen in a basic design."

"Many brides worry that fine linens are difficult to care for. On the contrary, they can easily be laundered at home, and because of their high quality, should last for years — but take care of stains immediately. Fine linens actually improve with age when treated well."

IMAGES OF LOVE

LONG AFTER THE WEDDING IS OVER, the photographs remain; whether taken by a talented friend or a seasoned professional, every photograph becomes only more precious with time. To tell the story of their wedding, most couples want a mixture of different styles: candid shots, posed shots, and portraits.

If you plan to hire a professional, interview several to select one whose style blends with yours. Meet well in advance of the wedding to fully discuss your expectations. Your wedding is a unique event, and you are closest to it ⁓ by all means, follow your instincts and your heart in making special requests for "must-have" photos.

Among the factors that determine the success of photographs, light is supremely important. The most flattering light is always at sunrise and sunset ⁓ the latter being the magic hour for wedding photographers. Family photographs taken at this time of day have a warm glow that resonates across generations. Discuss options such as candlelight versus overhead lighting with the photographer to achieve the most becoming images. Ask your photographer to visit the wedding site beforehand, at the same time of day.

If your wedding is at night, you will most certainly need flash photography, which could make the photographer more conspicuous as he or she attempts to capture spontaneous moments.

Remember, too, you don't necessarily have to limit yourself to black and white or color photos. Indoors, black and white film works well: It unifies colors and evens out flesh tones. Color is ideal outdoors when the landscape is monochromatic, as it is in the winter, or if the wedding takes place on a beach or near the water.

Interview

with a photographer MALLORY SAMSON

A wedding photographed by Mallory Samson always tells a special story. Here she explains her approach:

"I definitely believe in couples having a long meeting with the photographer before the wedding, just to chat about what they expect from their wedding and the photography. Once they're comfortable with each other, the photographer won't have an 'outsider's energy' at the wedding, which makes people freeze up."

"On assignments, I dress like a guest to blend in with the wedding party. Long lenses and small cameras help a photographer to quietly capture spontaneous candid shots."

"There are really two basic approaches to wedding photography, portrait and what I call intimate reportage photography. I see the wedding as a journey, with a beginning, middle, and end. There are the private moments, such as the bride getting ready, and public events like the reception. There are also literal pictures, emotional pictures, and detail pictures. A balance of them all makes a memorable album."

"The couple needs to let the photographer know in advance what's going to happen so he or she can capture every special moment. It's important to point out if there is anything unique to look for: hand-painted signs, a bridal arbor, an arrangement of family photographs, or a table offering handmade favors."

"Some couples want lots of photos of guests, others don't. Before the wedding day, they should make up lists of particular family photos they want to be taken, with names of guests who should be in them."

"In portraits the personalities of the bride and groom should shine through. For instance, the photo above shows a bride and groom kissing under a rose arbor. I didn't tell them to do this. I said, 'Show me how you feel right now' and a wonderful photograph just happened."

"After the honeymoon, couples are extremely excited to receive the photographs of their wedding day. It's a good idea for both the bride and groom to meet with the photographer and review the proofs. Based on this meeting, they can select the final photographs for printing, and the various sizes. In addition, couples should ask for their prints on the most long-lasting archival paper."

"Remember, having too many pictures is a good problem. Don't feel overwhelmed by the quantity before you. Ask your photographer's advice when you are ready to edit your selections. Photographers have a good deal of experience in telling a story through photos, and can help you make sound decisions that you will appreciate over the years. Later, if you do fall in love with another photograph, you can have that printed too."

WITH THIS RING

MORE THAN ANY OTHER SYMBOL, WEDDING rings tell the story of the heart. When a bride offers her left hand to her groom, it is the beginning of the journey of their married life together.

Brides have the whole history of the past to draw upon when selecting their rings. The family jewel box could well contain the ring you're searching for, but an estate jewelry hunt could also turn up your heart's desire. A fourteen-karat tricolor setting from the 1880s engraved with an orange blossom pattern would make a lovely choice indeed for an old-fashioned bride.

As early as the fifteenth century, diamonds delighted well-to-do brides. But other gemstones are popular for engagement rings, too: a lover of spring violets might consider amethyst, garnet, sapphire, tourmaline, and jadeite. For those who are true to blue, sapphire, aquamarine, and the more esoteric spinel, lapis lazuli, and topaz make for a cerulean repertoire. Green's rich hues find representation in emerald and peridot. For lovers of the winter holidays, ruby, garnet, and alexandrite celebrate the colors of the season.

When it comes to the marriage ring, a slender gold band to match the groom's is an eternally beautiful choice, but consider as well the charms of the ornamented ring. Blends of silver and gold (representative of sun and moon) express the union of bride and groom.

There are countless jewelers who will design rings to your specifications. Combinations of colors and textures are especially pleasing: for instance, a braided band of apricot gold, or a tricolor band featuring rose and white gold. Handcarved foliage or engraving on the outer side of the band are other lovely possibilities.

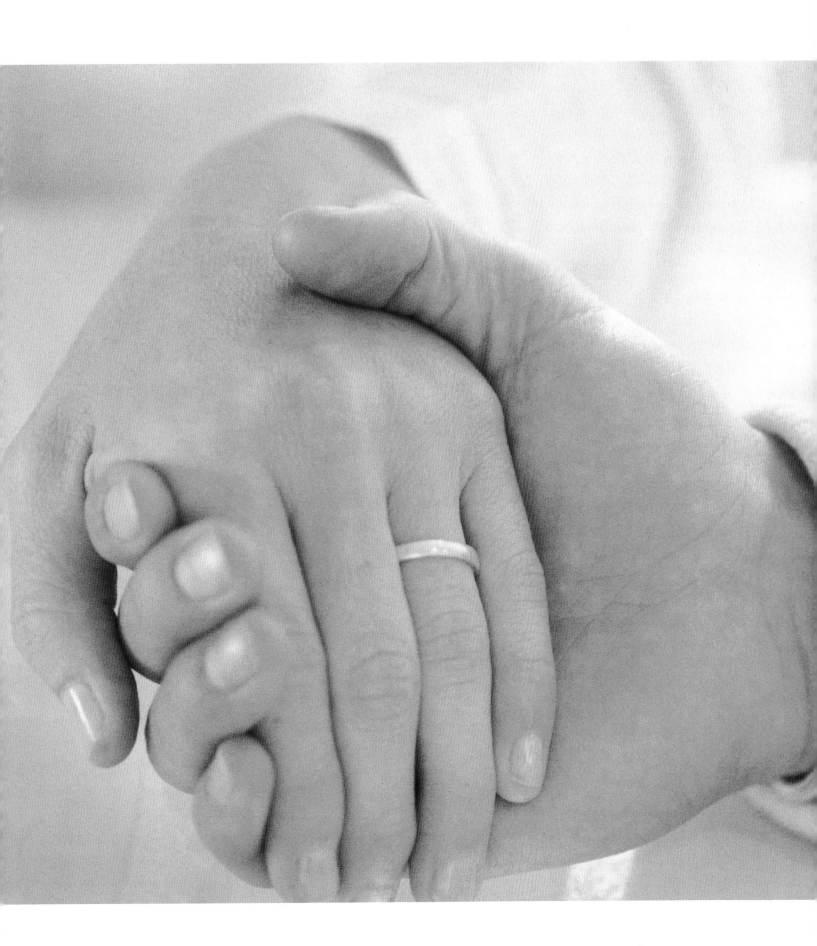

Old, New, Borrowed, and Blue

Enduring customs are part of the romance of weddings. No matter how sophisticated brides may be, there is one superstition they all seem to observe. What does this beloved custom mean?

♥ SOMETHING OLD Weddings are an important rite of passage; an old piece of jewelry or family Bible symbolizes the bride's connection to her past.

♥ SOMETHING NEW The bride journeys from her old life to her new one, with a token of her future — something new to ensure prosperity.

♥ SOMETHING BORROWED Long ago it was deemed lucky for a bride to borrow something from a happily married woman — to borrow a bit of her good luck. Costly veils were the favorite "Something Borrowed."

♥ SOMETHING BLUE Since the days of the biblical Hebrews, blue has been a color associated with spiritual loyalty and devotion.

♥ AND A SILVER SIXPENCE IN HER SHOE Brides, please note: Two major symbols of wedded life combine here. The sixpence (or in America, a dime) represents future wealth, and the shoe is an ancient symbol of authority.

BRIDAL FINERY

*T*ucked in a corner of every woman's heart is a vision of herself dressed for her wedding day, the way she wants to look and to feel. Perhaps it's your secret dream to glide down the aisle like a ballerina, caressed in yards of fluttering tulle, crowned with a halo of roses; or to emerge resplendent as a winter bride, cossetted in luxurious velvet complete with a muff; or to take vows wearing a much treasured family heirloom. The variety of bridal ensembles is thrilling, and just as you found the perfect man to marry, you will find the perfect look for your wedding day.

More than any other element, the bride's gown and her headpiece determine the image of the wedding ～

from her aura all else follows: the

design of the flowers, what the

attendants will wear, even the groom's suiting. On this

glamorous occasion, you as the bride are permitted extravagance. Enjoy the

luxury as piece by piece you select your romantic gown,

veil, jewelry, gloves, and slippers. Think of your appear-

ance as a whole rather than as the

separate elements, and enrobe

yourself in the finest. Indulge in silky

lingerie and brand-new toiletries,

adorn your tresses with antique combs or rosebuds, and buy

the string of pearls you have always wanted. It's your day.

ONE PERFECT GOWN

ONCE A WOMAN SLIPPED INTO HER best Sunday dress for her wedding, borrowed a veil, and gathered a bouquet from her garden. But one hundred and fifty years ago, a young Queen Victoria forever changed that: She married her prince wearing a romantic white floor-length gown with a full flowing veil. So beautiful was this regal image that from that day on brides have embraced the all-white wedding.

The bridal ensemble has gone off into many lovely directions, and there truly is the dream look for every bride, whether it is a family heirloom, a designer gown, or something she makes herself. With so much to choose from ⸺ elaborate lace confections, slender silk sheaths, traditional ballgowns, and classic wedding suits ⸺ the options can at first seem daunting.

Yet most designers ⸺ and brides looking back with the gift of hindsight ⸺ would agree that following the maxim "to thine own self be true" is best. Rely on your sense of what looks best on you, and what will make you feel special yet relaxed. There are a few basic guidelines: The more formal the wedding, the more luxurious the gown. Customary for the most formal event are full-skirted gowns with trains and fitted bodices ⸺ the A-line and the ball gown in rich fabrics such as silk, satin, or brocade ⸺ and headpieces with long veils. A semi-formal gown is floor-length and worn with a fingertip veil, while an informal look can be a dress or a suit of any length.

Fabrics simply follow the seasons in logical fashion: in spring and summer airy chiffon, organza, or crisp linen; the autumn bride in taffeta or silk shantung; in winter, rich velvet or silk damask, or even ivory cashmere.

Interview

with a **gown designer**
HELEN MORLEY

English-born designer Helen Morley has a contemporary, young vision that she brings to her classically shaped styles. Renowned for fine couture touches, her gowns are perfect for the romantic bride.

"The most important point about a wedding gown is how it fits. A bride must see what flatters her. For instance, while you may admire the gown opposite for is its immaculate rows of pleats (each one is edged in French ribbon), the true genius comes in its slimming dropped-waist bodice."

"For such an important purchase, go to a salon with a good reputation. Remember, you will be working with them for about six months from first visit to final fittings. Putting yourself in the hands of experts is a good way to reduce stress."

"Brides always say they want something elegant and simple, which sounds like no embellishment of any kind. They've confused simple with plain — which is exactly the opposite of what a bride should be on this, the loveliest day in her life. Embellishment doesn't have to come in fussy form; it can be a part of the construction of the dress. For instance, a crisscross of pleats across the bodice creates an interesting interplay of lines, yet the effect is understated."

"Since choosing a gown is not easy, you will probably want another opinion. It's a good idea to bring in a friend or relative after you've edited

your choices down to three or four. Ask someone who knows you want your gown, not hers."

"Think twice before commissioning an original gown. Ready-made gowns designed by bridal specialists have been worked through many, many prototypes: Their fit and flow have been proven perfect, and the gowns move with the bride up staircases and in and out of cars. They have been painstakingly designed to be flattering in photographs as well as in person."

"I find that brides today are very informed, and they are eager to learn more. A good salon will provide guidance on all the bridal accessories, including the bride's jewelry, and for the wardrobe of the wedding party."

"Think of the wedding gown as a single part of a whole: One of my favorite looks is a sleek sheath topped by an organza overcoat. Somehow, the effect is both old-fashioned yet fashion-forward, and it works well for formal and semi-formal brides, at afternoon and evening weddings."

"Base your choice of dress on the size you are when you place your order for it. Resist the impulse to put extra pressure on yourself to slim down — most brides automatically lose a little weight before a wedding, and every gown is always tailored to fit by the salon, even close to the day of the ceremony."

The Ballgown

With its fitted bodice and waist and generous skirt, a formal ballgown is decidedly regal. For such a traditional dress, the more sumptuous the fabric, the better: lustrous satin for winter, ethereal silk chiffon for summer, layered skirts of tulle and taffeta all year round. The flourishes are best kept simple, like bows made from the same material. Also for the most formal events, brides accent sleeveless or short-sleeved gowns with long, dramatic gloves.

A bride holds the skirts of her gown delicately (opposite), gathering the layers of fabric in soft folds between her hands. Lifting the skirts this way enables her to glide gracefully down a staircase or to ascend the steps of a waiting carriage or limousine.

Interview

with a restoration expert
ELAINE HARTLEY

Words of wisdom from designer and restorer Elaine Hartley, whose skilled hands transform vintage clothing into glorious wedding finery at Paris 1900 in Santa Monica, California:

"If you have an heirloom gown that you'd like to wear on your wedding day but it requires alterations, seek out the services of a professional experienced in the construction of period garments. Try your local historical society or a costume institute for help in locating an expert."

"Good candidates for alterations are gowns made from linens and cottons. These materials are surprisingly durable. Silks, cashmeres, and woolens tend to deteriorate, but you can often save their wonderful trimmings: netting, laces, ribbons, beading, or buttons, to ornament a new gown."

"With vintage clothing, brides have the opportunity to put together an ensemble of different elements. This works especially well in shades of white: For example, a hand-embroidered linen A-line walking skirt from 1910 worn with an Armistice blouse with a front edged in filet lace, and even a cotton piqué man's vest from the '20s would look ultra-romantic."

"Keep in mind that in the past, dresses were intended to be worn with a corset, according to the style of the time. During the Civil War, shoulders were narrow, sleeves and bodices tight. Women couldn't lift their arms — and there was

little extra material. From the late Victorian through the early Edwardian periods, corsets took on a different shape, more of an "S," and this resulted in billowing material in the front, shortwaisted backs, and tiny waists. Clothes from these periods are excellent candidates for re-sizing because the extra material in the front can be removed and used elsewhere."

"A lot of antique gowns have high collars and long, tight sleeves, making them uncomfortable to wear, but they're made from beautiful materials. The embroidery, laces, and cottons are so superior to what is available today that it's worth working them into another style of dress ⁓ perhaps by scaling back the sleeves, trimming the neckline, or adding inserts at the seams."

"As a preserver, I never advocate tearing apart a spectacular antique gown. If it is in excellent condition, preserve it for its historic value. But when you have only the elements of a gown, for instance a beautiful bodice with a worn-out skirt, try pairing it with a new, complementary skirt."

"Decades ago, brides had keepsake charms and ribbons sewn into the hems of their gowns for good luck. Ask your seamstress to keep an eye out for these, and perhaps you could add a charm of your own ⁓ a lock of your groom's hair with a lock of your own, or a ribbon or button from an outfit of special significance to you both."

Formal Gowns

Studded with tiny pearls and rhinestones, a traditional tulle-skirted ballgown (left) takes on the glamour appropriate for an evening wedding, particularly in the heart of winter. Splendid in the beauty of yesteryear, a modern bride will look magnificent in a gloriously preserved, abundantly laced gown (opposite). The fitted bodice and ruffled neckline are among the most flattering silhouettes, and ethnic touches such as a Highland sash make the gown interesting. Attendants follow the bride's lead in finery.

VEILED IN BEAUTY

A BRIDE WALKS DOWN THE AISLE with her veil floating about her like moonglow. As she leaves the church on the arm of her new groom, the lifted veil reveals her first dazzling smile as a married woman. How can we help but feel a catch in our throats?

A tradition thousands of years old, the veil does much to enhance a bride — it shows off a beautiful back by just skimming her shoulders, or it lends balance to the silhouette of a bride in a fitted gown. Swept upward in an elegant style, a veil frames the face. Paired with a tiny crown tiara, the veil brings its bride a regal stature. Tiaras and headbands can also mirror the season or style of the dress — seed pearls or tiny porcelain flowers enchant on a spring day.

Today, the selection of veils is abundant, from simple swaths of tulle piped in satin to the ultimate in formality and sheer volume: the cathedral veil, trailing for at least nine feet. You may find the perfect veil waiting for you in a family chest: panels of antique lace to transform into a romantic mantilla, or Great-grandmother's handmade Honiton lace veil. In the past, borrowing a veil was thought to bring good luck to the bride; happily, veils do not go in and out of style.

For the less formal wedding, a hat coupled with a veil makes a romantic showing. A length of tulle added to a portrait hat or soft netting to a high tea hat adds fantasy without formality.

Many brides forego the veil altogether and look beautiful with only a crown of flowers. To emphasize a bride's face, a bloom or two caught up in a comb or nestled in a French braid is a lovely alternative. The full garland, with or without a veil, is the most classic headdress of all.

A Wisp of Lace

A crown of white flowers has distinguished brides for generations. Whether the flowers are gently molded into a halo, a garland, a coronet, or a Juliet cap, their very fragility symbolizes the freshness of the wedding vows. To create the headpiece, each flower must be individually wired. Attaching the veil, whether of antique lace or tulle netting, is best left to the experienced hands of a milliner. Once in place, the flowers and veil are worn for the ceremony; before the reception, the veiling may be removed and safely stored.

Summer brides are blessed with more than wonderful weather: The temperate climate affords them the opportunity to wear light, diaphanous fabrics in delicate, short-sleeve styles. For these brides, an artless veil is often the best. Even one made from several yards of antique lace need not be elaborate: it can be draped over the bride's head, tossed over her shoulder, and held in place with a single yet perfect hydrangea. The magnificence of the lace is matched by the glory of the flower and the panache of the bride.

Perfectly Matched

Beyond considerations of face shape and hairstyle, a headpiece must complement the bride's gown. An embroidered net gown is classically paired with a beaded headband, every bit its equal in airy glamour (opposite). For the most formal gowns, lavishly encrusted with pearls and beads, a structured cap appropriately bejeweled is a good counterpart (right). With both headpieces, simple tulle netting is best.

An Interview

with a milliner TIA MAZZA

Designer of custom veils and head-pieces, Tia Mazza creates dazzling, head-turning looks that crown brides. She offers insights borne of her many years' experience:

"Veils are enjoying a resurgence in popularity. A bride may be convinced that she doesn't want a veil, until she tries one on. Suddenly she realizes: It's my wedding, and this wonderful bridal tradition makes me look so romantic. Not only does the veil rivet all eyes on the bride, it photographs so beautifully."

"Most any item can be worked into a headpiece as long as it's small and delicate: silk flowers, glass beads, pearls, crystals, or even a family brooch."

"While there are many different looks for veils, the standard lengths — blusher (elbow length), fingertip, and cathedral — can be made to be detached from the headpiece during the reception if the bride wishes."

"The veil and headpiece should echo the style of the wedding, as well as the bride's gown and her hairstyle. A veil with a long train would not work well in a garden wedding or a tiny chapel, but a long veil would be glorious going down the aisle in a cathedral. Heavy headpieces with long veils are difficult to control outdoors."

"When trying on veils and headpieces, try to wear a top with a neckline like your gown and your hair close to the style you will have on the big

day, even though you will probably take your veil and headpiece to the hairdresser for a final styling. Well-made headpieces and veils are fitted with wire combs and loops. A good hairdresser knows how to work with them and will secure them carefully."

"When matching a veil to your gown, look at the decorative details of the gown and have these elements echo, very subtly, in the headpiece."

"If a bride wants to wear an heirloom lace veil but finds its length a bit overwhelming, she should consider gathering it in the middle on a comb, so that it drapes softly."

"Rather than covering a veil with rhinestones,

which tend to look like black spots in photos, consider crystals, which reflect light."

"Brides always ask me how to best steam their veils on their wedding day. I tell them to just use a blow dryer set on warm, not hot."

"I like to use thin wire combs on my headpieces instead of a barrette or plastic comb, which never adequately hold the headpiece secure."

"With my trademark veil, the 'Tia Veil,' I achieve a flattering waterfall illusion by cutting and gathering the veil to maximize fullness and height."

LITTLE GEMS

TO COMPLETE HER ENSEMBLE, A BRIDE searches for the perfect accessories. In addition to the traditional pearls, there are so many beautiful things to be worn. If you have a love of jewelry, what better time to indulge your passion than now? At a daytime wedding, jewelry has an understated air: perhaps simple gemstone earrings with a delicate velvet choker, an antique locket, or a cameo. Formal dress occasions and evening ceremonies call for sophisticated touches: a Victorian-style mesh collar and pearl drop earrings are elegant choices. In a country setting, what could be sweeter than a silk ribbon tied about your neck? A wedding is an occasion to dip into the family jewelbox for pins, bracelets, brooches, earrings, necklaces, and lockets. In Victorian times, brides often wore a piece of jewelry set with the birthstone of the groom, a lovely custom worth reviving. Some lucky brides receive a "welcome into the family" gift, a most thoughtful expression of love.

For this emotional event, every bride needs a lace handkerchief. To hold one, a small bag is most useful, perhaps an antique reticule or a beaded bag, or a simple drawstring pouch made with a piece of antique lace.

the poetry of pearls

OF ALL THE JEWELS ASSOCIATED WITH weddings, pearls have a special place in the hearts of brides. For a woman in Victorian times, a string of pearls, presented by her fiancé, was the ultimate declaration of love: lustrous, hand harvested, and extremely costly, pearls were much cherished jewels, and they were carefully protected in silk-lined velvet boxes.

Victorians embraced the beauty of pearls, and wealthy ladies measured their esteem by the number of pearls in their necklaces. The dazzling figure above belonged to Edith Kingdon Gould, a celebrated actress of the Belle Epoque shown displaying a wealth of pearls from New York's famed establishment, Tiffany's.

While still highly prized today, most pearls do not command astronomical sums as in the past.

Starting in the 1920s, more affordable cultured pearls were developed. Soon, pearls became the darlings of fashion designers such as Parisienne Coco Chanel, who used them in abundance in her jewelry and on her fashion.

The favorite of poets and writers alike, these romantic jewels represent a lovely custom, appearing in countless forms on wedding day. Perhaps you've been fortunate enough to inherit a family heirloom such as a cameo framed in seed pearls, a pearl choker, or drop earrings. Or you may be commemorating the start of your new life with a special piece from a favorite jeweler or an antiques shop. Whatever way you wear them on your wedding day, pearls not only magnify the glow from your radiant face, they continue a beloved wedding tradition

Hand in Glove

Be they lacy hand-crocheted cotton or opera length kid leather, gloves and the bride have enjoyed a long fashion alliance. Up until the middle of this century, gloves were considered the finishing touch to a lady's every ensemble — especially for an event as important as a wedding, and brides in their wisdom have retained this stylish accessory. For every wedding there is a glove that whispers "elegance," whether the ceremony is early in the day or after the moon climbs above the trees.

Sentimental Edwardian brides often embroidered the groom's initials or wedding symbols on gloves of leather and cotton, a lovely tradition worth adopting on a new pair of gloves, family heirlooms, or a special find from an antiques shop.

When selecting your gloves, look for those that promise comfort as well as elegance —

the right length, height, and fabric are starting points. Long regarded as supremely comfortable, gloves of napa leather lend a hand to the bride on this special day of reception lines and dances; this leather is supple and light, making it feel good nearly year-round, especially when silk-lined for extra comfort. Its refined elegance is lovely combined with ornamented or opulent gowns. Crocheted gloves or those fashioned from lace heighten the femininity of a tailored wedding ensemble such as a sheath or wedding suit.

Who could anticipate such delicacy in leather? Who could expect the harmony between leather and organza? Wrist-length, two-button gloves (opposite) can become the bride's most dramatic touch, drawing all attention to the movements of her lovely hands. For a simple summer wedding, the winsome crochet glove can carry any style gown, and works well for every member of the bridal party (above). Most elegant, most dramatic, tailored opera-length gloves complement the long, slender lines of a tabard of antique beaded lace over a satin slip dress (right).

Gloves have a terminology all their own. When shopping, brides learn that gloves are identified by button length whether they have buttons or not: mid-wrist being two button, four-buttons reaching to the mid-forearm. Long-stemmed opera-length gloves stretch to the upper arm, while their opposite, demure "wristy" or "palm vent" gloves are the shortest, just touching the wrist, at the bride's pounding pulse point.

Romantic Steps

The matter of shoes is very close to women, and no less so the bride. Once you have your gown, look for shoes complementary in style and sophistication. As with your headpiece, you may want to repeat a design element on the shoe. Because there are so many shades of white, shoes can be dyed to match the fabric of your gown exactly. Comfort, too, is a real concern: From gliding up the chapel aisle to twirling on the dance floor at the reception, you may be walking on air, but you'll still be on your feet all day. For many, the solution is a comfortable silk or satin pump. Look for details such as a shaped back to make a heel appear more graceful, handsewn stitches, and embroidered fabrics. Another pretty option is the ballet-type shoe, in plain white leather or satin, lavished with lace and ribbons. Fine "party slippers" glide out of the house and into the ballroom with ease, and are supremely comfortable.

Some brides want to marry in pumps, then switch to party slippers or ballet shoes for the reception. And pumps, while lovely indoors, are not practical for an outdoor wedding, whether it is in the garden or at the shore.

Hand-embroidered slippers and shoes pay honor to the exacting detail that has gone into bridal fashion for hundreds of years. Antique shoes are available at many vintage clothiers, but alas, women of earlier generations seem to have had quite tiny feet. Modern shoemakers are happy to draw on their inspiration, though, and there are many styles and heel heights available. A wispy lace shoe looks impossibly fragile, but its sinuous yet sturdy heel actually provides a great deal of comfort (top left). A satin demi-heel with a single strap can move gracefully from the ceremony to the dance floor (bottom left). With its silk embroidery in differing shades of white, it is suitable for gowns in a number of tones. Of course, the first shoes brides wore were slippers, and they are still utterly romantic, particularly with pearls and ribbon embroidery (above). Whatever your shoes, do wear them at home several times before the wedding, to ensure they will be utterly comfortable. If they need any adjustment, seek a shoemaker experienced with these delicate materials.

Handmade Shoes

IF YOU WERE TO STEP INTO A WEDDING ceremony from long ago, you might be surprised by the bridal attire: Not only would brides travel down the aisle in gowns of every color — blue, gray, lavender, and plum were favorite choices — but their bridesmaids wore finery to match. Even the rare bride who did wear a white gown might be preceded by an all-white entourage, for virtually as much attention was lavished on the bridesmaids' dresses as on the bridal gown.

This custom came about for a practical reason. Only the most well-to-do brides indulged in the luxury of the "one-time-only" dress. As part of one's wardrobe, an expensive dress had to be versatile enough for many functions.

As customs come full circle, bridesmaids are reclaiming their stylish roles in the wedding. They seek out flattering special-occasion wear that can be worn again and again, and they do not limit themselves to the "bridesmaids section" of a shop. For daytime, linen has few peers — a sheath topped with a cropped jacket or an elegant cashmere sweater is a stylish choice. Even white ensembles for bridesmaids have returned: a swirly skirt paired with a lacy ivory blouse, sashed at the waist with a wide gingham ribbon, is charming at an informal garden wedding. For evening glamour, a scatter of crystal beads might twinkle on a chiffon shawl worn over an organza dress.

The notion that all attendants dress alike has softened too. While it's best if gowns are similar in silhouette and share a color palette, there is no need for everyone to wear totally identical necklines, shoes, and headpieces. Some brides even encourage their attendants to choose bouquets composed of their own favorite flowers.

Angels in Tulle

Bridesmaids and honor attendants dressed in complementary but decidedly unidentical gowns each shine. To keep harmony in the face of individuality, the palette is kept simple and the fabrics similar. Swells of pastel tulle skirts and matching shawls share the same silhouette, completely feminine and classically constructed. The fitted bodices may be halter top, v-neck, or ballerina, a decision to be made by the bride and each attendant. For the wedding, these bridesmaids will carry tussie-mussies made of different kinds of flowers, but of the same size.

FEW BRIDES RESIST HAVING CHILDREN in their wedding parties. Children ⌒ especially girls ⌒ adore weddings, mesmerized by the sheer splendor and pageantry of the event. The ideal flower girl age ranges from four to eight, with junior bridesmaids from eight to fourteen.

For every season, there is a captivating flower girl outfit. Spring brings lined organdy dresses with scalloped Peter Pan collars and lavish sashes, while summer's smocked dresses trimmed with silken florets can't help but lend enchantment to the occasion. Borrow a page from the past: A Victorian-style white muslin dress with white stockings and sash are winsome any time of the year, while white velvet with a red woolen coat for Christmas couldn't be more festive.

Should you have many flower girl candidates, don't limit yourself to one ⌒ follow a European tradition and surround yourself with a flock of flower girls. Their dresses need not be identical; you could contrast shades of white and soft pastels, or vary the colors of their sashes and shoes, or flowers. Because the dresses are small, seamstresses lavish on the details, whether they are sweet bands of floral embroidery or bows of satin and silk ribbons.

To ensure happiness throughout the event, flower girls must feel special, yet comfortable, and their dresses are best made from loose-fitting, light fabrics. Shoes should be sensible as well as adorable: Mary Janes and ballerina slippers will make her feel like a princess. The most successful headpieces are simple, perhaps a halo of miniature roses or a satin bow. Just be sure that any headpieces are well fastened; we all know how much flower girls love to twirl in their special dresses.

Charms of the Past

If you're in love with the romance of the past and would like to dress your flower girl in an antique dress, a trip to a vintage clothing shop could yield a treasure. Earlier in this century, white linen and cotton clothing was central to a girl's wardrobe. Because they were made from sturdy fibers, many dresses, blouses, and skirts have survived beautifully and are ready to return to their place in the sun. Not only are they hand-washable, but often they can be mended or restored by a professional. When searching for the perfect dress, keep alterations in mind, and look to the larger sizes as well: A highly tailored, fitted tea dress intended for a high school girl on her graduation day at the turn of the century is likely to be too small for a girl of the same age today, but it easily may be altered for a younger, modern-day flower girl. Even antique cotton nightgowns, so exquisite with their hand-sewn details and tiny pearl buttons, can be lined and altered. If you're a talented seamstress or have the services of one, patterns are available for turn-of-the-century children's clothes from mail order companies.

Flower girls are as distinctive as the brides they serve. When a pair of flower girls is present (especially when they are twins) their costumes can vary just slightly, with sashes of different fabrics, in different colors, so that guests can tell them apart. Or a flower girl may wear a gown inspired by the bride's own, repeating elements such as mutton sleeves and lace-trimmed bodices. Yet another option for flower girls, particularly for winter holiday weddings, is to add a waistcoat of contrasting fabric, even running to black velvet.

EVEN WITH ALL THE EXQUISITE CLOTHING and accessories you have assembled for your wedding day, nothing is more essential to your beauty than glowing good looks. The steps to achieve this are simple, but often elusive in the exuberant days before you enter what the poet Wendell Berry called "the country of marriage." Basically, they are rest, exercise, and time for yourself.

Beginning several months before the wedding, create a special beauty regime. Schedule time for skin-nurturing baths, both a way to unwind and to savor precious pre-wedding moments. Heighten this pleasure with soft music playing in the background and a scented candle flickering away. Today, herb shops offer a repertoire of dried botanicals and essential oils for every need: for instance, rosemary, mint, or rose or violet flowers to soothe, geranium and sandalwood for the pure delight of fragrance. Simply place a small handful of the herbs of your choice in a drawstring muslin bag, place it under the faucet, and let the bath fill with scented water.

If you prefer, keep a selection of bath oils and salts on hand, as well as talcs. Look for those redolent of orange blossoms, a scent ever touted for reducing stress and inducing sleep. Lavender has the same gentle effect, so fill a pretty cloth bag or handkerchief with dried blossoms and hang it from your bedpost to attract pleasant dreams. Do not overlook the power of tea as you drift off to sleep. A cup of linden, rosehip, or chamomile tea not only calms jangled nerves but helps to clarify the complexion. Just the ritual of brewing it will be soothing.

As part of your beauty regimen, take extra good care of your body and soul. For healthy hair

and nails, don't skip protein-rich meals, as difficult as it seems, and try to schedule more frequent salon visits. For inner beauty, take time to relish the uniqueness of all that is happening now; take long walks with your fiancé, discussing everything but the wedding.

The Bride's Dressing Room

On her wedding morning, a bride needs to surround herself with the utmost beauty, starting with a luxurious dressing area. Before this most special day, equip the space with a pair of full-length mirrors (which you can rent from an antiques shop) and pile on the amenities: plush, deep fluffy bath towels, a gorgeous dressing gown, padded hangers, and silk lingerie bags. Fill your vanity table with all the pleasures of a woman's toilette — powders and perfumes in your favorite scent. Buy beautiful brushes, a comb, and a mirror. Perhaps you've been lucky enough to have been given antique perfume bottles; if not, now is a good time to acquire some, and they'll look lovely in the intimacy of your new bedroom.

As delicate as the first breeze of spring, a silk organza nightdress is the stuff of wedding-night dreams. Tiny beads, the only embellishment, rim the neckline (left). A bustier of boned lattice-work and net scalloped lace can make all the difference in the way a wedding dress looks, and is best fitted by a professional (above). For honeymoon evenings spent entirely au chambre, *a drift of Honiton and Brussels lace with a lace top falling over the skirt cel-ebrate a new intimacy (opposite).*

HEAVENLY BEAUTY

APART FROM HER WEDDING GOWN AND veil, no aspect of appearance is dearer to a bride's heart than the way her hair looks on her wedding day. In recent years, we seem to have reversed an older custom of wearing hair loose, as brides sweep up their locks into styles that reveal a beautiful neck and face. To achieve a classic, flattering look

that complements an elegant ensemble, hair experts advise choosing a hairstyle that's simple and natural looking, yet more sophisticated than an everyday one. Ideally, the bride will have a trim a month in advance and highlights if necessary — especially if her hair is swept into a classic updo, in which the underside of the style trades places with the top and becomes more eye-catching.

Whether you choose a tailored French twist, or a pinned-up look with face-framing tendrils loose at the neck and forehead, experiment well in advance of your wedding day to settle on the ideal style to complement your dress. Chignons elegantly set off high necklines, while French twists complement dresses that expose back or shoulders. Many hairstyles are so pretty they don't need a headpiece: instead frame the face with small blossoms. As with any bridal flowers, evaluate the

blooms for durability, choose flowers that last, such as miniature orchids and stephanotis, and eschew those that fade quickly, like pansies and violets. To dress up short hair, clips and barrettes look special and hold flowers, such as a glamorous gardenia or a sprig of white hyacinths.

Belle Visage

To show your finest face this day, you deserve to treat yourself to the best, and this is true for cosmetics as well as lingerie and flowers. Because you will be seen in many types of light — daylight, indoor light, flash-bulb light — your make-up has to give you a nonstop, glowing appearance. Photographers who specialize in weddings are expert sources of information on make-up for the camera, as are beauty consultants. Discuss this with them beforehand to be sure your make-up is seamless and perfect — with your face, neck,

bodice, and shoulders looking their smooth best.

With so many meetings and greetings ahead, you'll want high-quality cosmetics that last as long as possible. For this reason, many brides seek the services of a beauty professional to to ensure a flawless experience. Other brides prefer doing their own make-up. Whichever you choose, a wedding allows you the luxury of purchasing some of the cosmetics and accoutrements you've always dreamed of: soft blushes, powders, elegant lip and nail colors, fine natural brushes and puffs.

Match the degree of make-up to the formality and time of the ceremony, yet always remain natural-looking. Candlelight evening ceremonies call for more drama and color, while garden weddings require a lighter touch on cheeks and lips. For touch-ups, your maid-of-honor can carry a small cosmetic pouch for you.

Interview

with a beauty expert GUI VRABL

A bride made up by Gui Vrabl is always the most beautiful woman at the wedding. Here he shares his secrets for success.

"Some brides do their makeup themselves, or have a sister or friend try it, but, if there's one day in a woman's life when she wants to be at her loveliest, it's her wedding day. The greatest favor a bride can do herself is to engage the services of an expert make-up artist and hair stylist. This way, much of the tension and guesswork is removed well before the ceremony, and the bride knows she'll look wonderful in person and in photographs."

"The bride should schedule a pre-wedding consultation about a month in advance. She can run through her options then, without a lot of deadline pressure, and discuss making last-minute adjustments, such as highlighting or a haircut for shape. If the bride wants a major change, this is the time for it, not right before the wedding."

"The bride, or the makeup artist, should decide which is her stronger feature: lips or eyes, and then emphasize only one. For example, beautiful, defined lips are paired with soft eyes, and striking eyes with a subtle mouth. Soft, tender color is best for wedding make-up. Softer tones in blusher, foundation, and lipstick are ideal for brides of any skin color."

"Every aspect of her wedding day appearance should be discussed: photography, lighting, wedding location, what to do for any last-minute emergencies — break-outs, broken nails, humid or rainy weather. It's also critical for the consultant to see the bridal head piece and gown to have a total vision of the image the bride wants. The fail-proof approach is to have a trial run, a full dress rehearsal. Have your hair and make-up done, then dress. Look for comfort, ease of movement, and appearance from front and back. Sit, dance, shake your head to be sure you will look beautiful throughout the reception."

"Unless she has very short hair, I usually advise that the bride wear her hair up — whether in a chignon, French twist, or a bun. An up-swept style shows off the bride's face and neck, and it has a more practical benefit: She doesn't have to worry

during her wedding day. I might also work with the florist to place a few small buds in the hair."

"In the end, the bride's state of mind will show through. I strongly advise setting aside the entire day before the wedding to relax and be pampered. Perhaps visit a spa with a friend — but no facials within four days of the wedding (to avoid any redness). This day of calm, away from all the inevitable last-minute crises that usually solve themselves anyway, will pay her back many times over when she is finally dressed, made up, and absolutely radiant on her wedding day."

The Wedding Bouquet

After the wedding gown, the bride's flowers are probably the most ethereal element of the wedding. When we think of wedding flowers, roses often come first to mind, and certainly they are prized for their supreme beauty. Yet another flower, the orange blossom, has an even longer association with the bride. "She is to wear the orange blossom," promised many a 19th-century engagement announcement. As fine as lace and as fragrant as precious perfume, this coveted white flower is perhaps the most traditional choice of all, having been carried by brides for two thousand years.

When planning the wedding flowers, usually the bride starts with her own bouquet and proceeds from there to any flowers she may want for her hair. Then she selects those for her wedding party: garlands or baskets of posies for flower girls, depending on the formality of the wedding. While on her wedding day a bride is free to select any flowers, most often, formal bouquets are all white with white ribbons; they can be arm-size cascades, or smaller bouquets.

The nosegay and fuller bouquets appear with equal elegance at the semiformal ceremony. Combinations of pastels or simply creamy-toned flowers are lovely here.

Informal bouquets can be anything from tiny tussie-mussies gathered into antique metal holders, globe-like pomanders of a single flower, large bouquets of mixed flowers, or a jumble of wild flowers straight from a meadow.

Tides of fashion may change the look of the bridal bouquet, but there is one rule that will always endure whether you engage the services of a floral designer or use your own talents: Select the

Brides have a dazzling number of flowers to select from, too many to choose just one. Combining three seasonal flowers in a simple ring bouquet is one good solution: creamy tulips in the center, a ring of cool muscari, and a base of ivory roses just bursting open (left). For another bride, a clutch of full-blown roses is trimmed with a ruff of hand-embroidered lace (above). Even a tailored bride can carry a cascade, provided it has a casual, just-picked appearance. By including sprigs of herbs, ivy, and ferns (opposite), the bouquet bestows on the bride all the symbolic botanical elements of marital health and happiness.

flowers in season and a plentiful supply is yours. In springtime, hyacinths and bleeding-hearts, muscari, tulips, and peonies gently tint garden and woodland. You might mix them, but single-note bouquets, like a nosegay of lilies of the valley or a tumble of lilacs, are both simple to create and beautiful to behold. At the height of summer, a veritable floral symphony awaits: larkspur, Queen Anne's lace, and roses of every variety, for example. A trip to a cutting garden might yield astilbes, delphiniums, lilies, and sweetpeas, to mass into an arm-held cascade bouquet, the long, dramatic stems gathered with a generous double-face satin bow. Autumn brings a textural mix of hydrangea, asters, dahlias, and plumed grasses. For a seasonal palette, consider a blend of coral-toned roses, miniature yellow calla lilies, and russet viburnum berries. While Southern brides might carry a

densely packed nosegay of white hydrangeas paired with pale roses in autumn, those in cooler climes pick pink-green hydrangea paniculata joined by the last roses of the season in shades of deep burgundy and burnt orange. Even in winter's depths, both the Christmas rose (also called helleborus) and true roses fill the florist shop and look dramatic with evergreens like ivy, pine, and cedar. Winter berries, such as holly and the porcelain-white snowberry, are striking in a lushly scented bouquet of forced bulbs such as freesia.

White flowers of any kind can be part of the bride's bouquet. Held together by their pure ivory tones, roses, hyacinths, and astilbe beautifully blend their fragrances (above). Their stems are wrapped in a long piece of wide silk ribbon, which is tied in a bow at the neck of the bouquet. A pearl stickpin at the center of the bow holds it in place. Ribbon can play a major design role in even a lavish bouquet. By playing off the harmony of the warm white and green tones of tulips and roses, a peach grosgrain ribbon offers an unusual counterpoint (right). Ribbons for bouquets should always be of the very best quality, for they can become keepsakes to pass on to future brides.

A simple spring bouquet (opposite) can be made of almost any blue and white flowers, including lilac, freesia, muscari, and periwinkle. A ring of shapely hydrangea leaves is a unifying element, and the stems are wrapped in white ribbon to finish the look.

Interview

with a floral designer
NICOLE ESPOSITO

A wedding by Nicole Esposito is characterized by the designer's extraordinary commitment to her brides. Believing that a bride's dreams should always come true, Nicole explains how to make this happen:

"Ideally, the floral design process begins with a 'get-acquainted' phone call five to six months before the wedding. Good communication is the key to success. A bride needs a designer who listens to her, whose style matches hers, and who genuinely cares. She should keep looking until she finds that. Professional designers always have photo books of their work — and can give you letters of recommendation."

"A face-to-face meeting gives the floral designer a fuller image of the bride, her style, and her goals. Most brides today are very knowledgeable about flowers and have an idea of what they want. Many bring along photographs they've collected: bouquets, headpieces, pretty tablesettings, for example. If a bride isn't sure what she wants, a good floral designer will work with her, refining her ideas, until she is happy."

"At that first meeting, lists are drawn up of all the flowers involved, from the bridal party bouquets to table arrangements, church decorations, and corsages. The more concrete a bride can be with the designer, the better. Fabric swatches from the gowns of the wedding party and color themes help make an even clearer picture."

"Don't hesitate to visit an 'expensive' designer even if your budget is modest. A real professional can help you focus on what's important, such as a beautiful bouquet, and will rise to the challenge of working with limited funds."

"If your budget is really modest, check to see if another wedding is scheduled to take place where yours will be. Brides can share the cost of church decorations, providing both weddings with more than one bride could afford on her own."

"Most designers prefer to visit the site of the ceremony and wedding in the company of the bride. The designer can make suggestions about finishing touches and the like — and decisions can be made on the site."

"Designers usually place orders for supplies three weeks, and for flowers one week, prior to the wedding day, so make any changes before that."

"Written delivery schedules are a must as the wedding day approaches; you need to know that everything is being taken care of. Carefully examine all the flowers as soon as they are delivered; your florist should be available for any repairs."

"Expect your designer to present you with a complete pricing agreement well in advance, usually within a week of confirming the arrangements. Don't hesitate to discuss changes at this point."

Freesia is a favorite for bridal flowers, in part due to its heavenly fragrance and its ability to stand up for hours without water. A great mass of it, surrounded by a ring of the deepest purple sweet peas and white euphorbia flowers, produces a bouquet ideal for the semi-formal or informal bride (right). After the ceremony, when her veil is removed, the bride can add sweet peas to her hair.

For a winter bride, deeply toned roses in shades of gold, pink, and crimson combine with blue lisianthus and white heather to echo the colors of a fine tartan (opposite). When the bride carries a bouquet of this magnitude, her attendants' flowers should be more modest, so that the event is not overwhelmed by flowers.

For the Party

Even when her attire strikes its own note, the bridesmaid's bouquet is often a floral allusion to that of the bride. If the bride carries a blend of orange blossoms, lilies of the valley, and poet's narcissus, for example, her maid's bouquet could also include orange blossoms, but with coral-colored ranunculus at its heart. Indulge in unexpected details: While the bride at a tartan wedding carries crimson roses with their foliage

for a green-and-red plaid theme, her maids strike a different note altogether with armfuls of heather. If the bride's arrangement is pale, accentuate her maids' with just a dash of color. Or let the color of the attendant's dress be the starting point for her flowers. If she wears blue, then her bouquet might cover the spectrum with pale forget-me-nots, royal blue muscari, veronica, annual larkspur, and pansies tied with a blue satin bow. Alternatively, blue delphiniums might encircle her waist or gather in a "bow" at her back. Remember the mothers of the bride and groom, too: Order flowers for both ⌒ perhaps a nosegay of one striking bloom, a wrist corsage, or a simple posy to tuck in a suit jacket pocket.

For the Flower Girls

Tiny fingers clasped tightly around a nosegay or tussie-mussie keep the flower girl's bouquet safely in position. From the simple bunch of lilies of the valley in an organdy ribbon (left) to an elaborate bouquet that includes orange blossoms, narcissus, rosebuds, and, for contrast, bright orange ranunculus (opposite), the only caveat is that the bouquet be small enough to hold comfortably.

THIS
FINE DAY

*Y*ou awaken on this day unlike any other, step from bed, and begin the

journey of your lifetime. Within hours, you'll be married and celebrating.

But right now, it's your wedding morning, and your pulse

is racing. The planning and the preparations are in place;

dozens of details have been anticipated and attended to.

All that's left is to experience every thrilling moment.

As you move through the day,

every emotion is heightened, bringing you close to tears

and laughter at every turn. In the company of loved

ones, you depart for the ceremony. Everything looks so

beautiful as you take your groom's arm ⌒ within

moments, you magically become husband and wife.

After the solemnity of

the service, you're ready to

celebrate. Spirits soar as rose petals fly through the air and the wedding party

heads off for the reception, where more of your dreams come true. Everything

is so romantic ⌒ music serenades you

as the moments slip by, candles glow,

wedding cakes tempt, and small children

dance shoeless. Before you know it, you're

tossing your bouquet and leaving for your

honeymoon. You're happy

that photographs will record every smiling face and blessing.

After the honeymoon, you'll have a lifetime to relive it.

WHEN A BRIDE ARRIVES FOR THE service, all the planning comes together. Now, she is a radiant bride, not a woman with hundreds of details to organize. This is her moment ⌒ indeed, this is her day ⌒ to shine.

Everywhere she looks, the results of her thoughtful decisions reveal themselves. For a church or synagogue wedding, the altar and aisle might be lined with flowers and herbs picked from the bride's garden that morning. Twin wreaths may hang from double doors, heralding the joy within.

If the ceremony is set at home or in a garden, built-in romance is a bonus. The garden is beautifully groomed; the tables and silver are polished and gleaming. Vows exchanged amidst beloved surroundings link couples with the past and future. Attendants, so beautiful in their special dress, stand faithfully by, happy to smile all day. Flower girls, their hair so sweet and fresh, remind guests of their own youths, when dreams of happiness like this first started.

The spell is unbroken as bride and groom speak their vows. Close friends step forward to recite a poem or to sing. As music swells and the bride and groom proceed from the ceremony, their path might be sweetened by rose petals or even sheaves of wheat, a tradition from the past thought to ensure prosperity.

If the reception is nearby, there is the delightful option of leading a procession through town to the site, a charming European custom that many American couples are choosing to adopt. If the distance is farther, a couple might ride in a Victorian-era horse-drawn carriage decorated with flowers, or motor along in a vintage car.

IN DAYS LONG-GONE, THE WEDDING feast was a highly spirited community event, with townsfolk celebrating for several days. While today's bride may not have to serve such a large number of guests, the feast ⌒ or reception ⌒ is still a much anticipated part of a wedding.

There are so many options for a romantic wedding meal. You could choose a bridal breakfast early in the day, a late-afternoon wedding tea with cake and Champagne, a more traditional sit-down dinner, even a clambake held at the shore. The most formal reception begins with bite-sized canapes and flutes of Champagne, butlered from beautifully decorated serving trays, followed by a seated, four-course meal. To crown this wedding dinner, servers will offer a light dessert, followed by slices of a glorious wedding cake. Such a multicourse feast is especially well produced in the ballroom of a large estate or a grand hotel.

The reception with a dinner served buffet-style is the next most formal reception. Guests are offered appetizers, then invited up to buffet tables. The dinner ends with the wedding cake, accompanied by one or two smaller desserts or fruit. For this celebration, a historic town house, a hotel, or a special space such as a museum or botanical garden with a well-equipped kitchen is a suitable choice.

Large or small, the informal reception is the most creative option of all. Here you can let your imagination soar ⌒ serve a variety of dishes from different cuisines or a selection of specialities prepared by friends and family, or mix and match foods under the direction of a caterer, who often sets up several serving tables from which guests select everything from appetizers to desserts.

The wedding cake is cut by the bride and groom, then sliced and served. This reception is especially charming for the bed-and-breakfast wedding, the garden party, and the at-home wedding.

When the reception is set outdoors, the magic is heightened all the more. Take your inspiration from French vineyard receptions: Cover the table with a simple linen cloth, top it with a fine lace runner, and set it with bowls of flowers.

Reception tables offer elaborate decorating possibilities: For a Christmas wedding, the pyramidal croquembouche dessert, the traditional wedding cake of France, makes a lovely appearance. Baskets heaped with strawberries in June look cool and appealing set atop a bed of strawberry leaves. Plates of lacy petit-fours nestle next to wedding favors such as sugar-covered almonds, contributing both a note of beauty as well as tradition. Cornucopias overflowing with the freshest garden vegetables and fruits not only symbolize the future prosperity of the bride and groom, they are delicious as well.

Some couples prefer to have their Champagne toast at the beginning of the reception, while others choose to toast when the wedding cake is served. "Here's To Happily Ever After!"

A Wedding at Home

Silver-framed brides of the past, heirloom linens

for the table, and the family's finest crystal: These

mark the home reception. Though the bride's

home is often the setting, this celebration is even

more heartfelt when the rooms are decorated with

mementoes of both the bride and the groom.

Home weddings are at their most romantic

when they are simple, whether there are a hundred

guests or a dozen. One glorious floral arrangement is

eye-catching; a lush swag of roses is all that's needed

to announce the bride's chair; a menu composed of

three or four favorites feels special. Of course, the

wedding cake can be as lavish as the bride's desire.

GARDEN WEDDINGS

Showing off her skills as the ultimate floral designer, Mother Nature sets the stage for the most romantic weddings. Trees, foliage, flowers, and sweeping lawns are the elements of this beautiful setting. Decide where you wish to exchange vows — in a gazebo, by a pond, or under a rose-covered trellis. For a shelter from strong sunlight, create a canopy of filmy

muslin or tulle, hung on sturdy lengths of bamboo that have been festooned with seasonal flowers and ivy.

For that fateful procession, many gardens offer natural aisles: a path edged by beds of perennials or hybrid tea rose bushes. You could fashion an aisle by lining up urns overflowing with herbs or pots of stately topiaries. Whimsy is the byword of a garden wedding — statues decked in rose garlands, containers tied with bows, gates hung with fresh wreaths or colorful flags.

Dining in a garden is always a treat. To create a country mood, float lengths of white eyelet or gingham atop tables; for more drama, organdy or creamy silk make a romantic canvas for silver and crystal. As dusk falls, Chinese lanterns and candles impart the romantic glow of a garden party from days gone by.

As you and your groom dance to the first notes of "your song," the time has finally come to have fun. Like fresh flowers, live music is all the more beautiful for its ephemeral quality ⌒ and happily, there are musical variations to suit every wedding. To set a sophisticated mood, tap the talents of a jazz trio with a vocalist who can render classics of Cole Porter and George Gershwin. For an intimate reception, a string quartet or a harpsichord and flute duet provide a hushed elegance. If you adore the close-knit feeling of a family reception, students from the local music academy could be engaged instead of a traditional band. Their fresh style imparts the air of a Victorian at-home wedding breakfast, where singers and pianists entertained and amateur performers ⌒ mostly a reliable ensemble of good-natured family members ⌒ gamely sang.

When your heart is set on dancing, guests can waltz to the music of an orchestra or a pianist, or swing to the sounds of a string trio. For large events, five- and seven-piece bands or large orchestras are especially fitting. To honor your old and new family, arrange for the music of both cultures to be played. Feet start tapping when bagpipes play a hearty Highland jig; tears well up when violins render a poignant ballad.

Because dancing at a wedding is irresistible fun, have enough space for both the musicians and the dancers, as well as the diners who enjoy watching this beautiful activity. If the reception takes place outdoors, under a large tent, ask for a generous dance floor. Several weeks before, prepare for your musicians a list of sentimental family favorites; at this emotional time, these melodies will be more welcome than ever.

FEW BRIDES FIND A RECEPTION SITE that is set up and perfect in every detail. Most often, it is the personal touches a bride brings to the reception that heighten its romance.

One of the easiest ways to subdue a room's atmosphere is with softer light. At late-day and evening receptions, candles placed everywhere ⟶ tapers and votives on guests' tables, pillars on a mantelpiece, candelabras on serving tables ⟶ cast a wonderful, flattering glow.

Talented brides find resourceful ways to transform the ordinary. When folding chairs wear slipcovers or seat cushions, receptions look tailored. When the stems of Champagne flutes are tied with slender bows, the toast is even more magical. Searching for serving pieces, many brides look to the opulent past, or raid the family's china closets. Nineteenth-century silver menu holders could hold calligraphed menu cards; filigree cake baskets look wonderful serving cookies or fruit, or offering favors to departing guests.

Tiny details are noticed, and even a table napkin need not be ordinary. It easily can be dressed up with a tiny sprig of honeysuckle or an autumn leaf, or caught up in a fat silk ribbon bow.

The Childrens' Table

Little ones mirror the excitement of a wedding. Long a part of the wedding, flower girls and ring bearers are often joined by other children at the reception. To make them feel more important, and to contain their high spirits to one area, prepare a table just for them. Have healthy snacks waiting for them upon their arrival, and easy-to-read place cards at their seats. For young children, you may need a table and chairs in their smaller size, if the reception site permits.

Receptions can seem to last forever to children, so provide activities to keep them busy: crayons and coloring books, disposable cameras, bottles of bubbles to add festivity to the air. Since children are not know for their patience, their food might be served on a separate schedule.

Interview

with a caterer
THOMAS PRETI

Receptions catered by Manhattan-based Thomas Preti evoke only superlatives. Here is his advice for ensuring the best of everything.

"Many couples think it's the number of guests at a wedding that determines a reception's cost, but it hinges more on where the wedding is held and whether or not the tables, chairs, dinnerware, and the like are provided."

"A first-rate caterer always makes sure a couple stays within their budget, and does not go unnecessarily overboard. When we first talk about their different options, I like to remind brides and grooms that the simplest celebrations are often the most elegant ones."

"Often couples want special dishes, a sentimental favorite or a family recipe, and a good caterer will work these requests into the menu. It's advisable to stay away from culinary high-wire acts such as soufflés, and from dishes that are risky with large crowds, such as some fish dishes and spicy foods."

"The reception site must be familiar to the caterer, and if not, visited. And the lighting and table design must be considered. Once all these elements are decided upon, a menu suited to the level of formality can be designed."

"Usually three percent of the wedding guests will be vegetarian, so it's good planning to have one special entrée made up in advance: perhaps an

elegant dish such as a sophisticated and substantial mushroom strudel, should a guest request an alternative."

"Rather than presenting guests with choices of entrées ∽ the classic chicken or fish ∽ we have found it worthwhile to serve a variety of smaller courses. That way there is something for everyone, even if a guest passes up one course. Today people do not want overly large portions, and this approach is far easier on the couple's budget."

"Once the bride and groom and the caterer have decided on a first-draft menu, the most fail-proof thing is to have a tasting. It's not enough to discuss a menu with a caterer ∽ even if you've sampled the company's food at another wedding or at its own restaurant."

"The engaged couple should sit down to a leisurely meal prepared by the caterer. This should replicate what their guests will experience at their wedding reception. The elements, including all the details, should be discussed ∽ the food, wine, breads, and dessert, all the way down to the chairs, china, silverware, and flowers. If a florist has already been chosen at this time, it is a good idea to have a sample centerpiece delivered to the tasting. Only then will a bride really rest assured that she's seen to every possible detail."

FLOWERS WEAVE MAGIC THROUGHOUT the reception: from the bride's and groom's chairs, to windows and staircases adorned with fragrant swags, to gorgeous tabletop arrangements.

While there may seem to be too many flower choices, as with every other element, the wedding's theme provides the direction for floral decorations. For more formal tabletop arrangements, you'll want an echo of the bride's bouquet, spread lower and wider to accommodate conversation and the scale of the table. For informal receptions, adorn the room with towering topiaries of fresh flowers that pick up the colors of a centerpiece, or fill urns with living branches. If the room has high ceilings, buy pre-made garlands of greens, which can be as large as seventy-five feet long, and wire on fresh flowers or dried leaves, depending on the season. Unusual containers for centerpieces could display the bride's style, or perhaps a passionate collection: blue and white Staffordshire nestled with roses, or Roseville vases overflowing with wisteria.

Remember too that the scent of table flowers is just as important as their beauty. Full-blown roses will weave an irresistible fragrance in the air while paperwhite narcissus may be too earthy for some. Flowers from a home cutting garden will likely have a lustier fragrance than their commercially grown counterparts.

In the flickering light of a candlelit reception, white and pastel flowers show up best. Peonies and lilacs are wonderfully romantic, as are stephanotis and hyacinths.

As party favors, few gestures are as charming as nosegays, each made with a few sprigs of flowers and tucked at the side of the plate.

the legacy of herbs

BEFORE THE LOVE-BESOTTED VICTORIANS TOOK OVER the language of flowers and herbs, brides and grooms were listening to these botanical messages. While flowers may reign supreme in matters of the heart, for centuries herbs have enjoyed a broader appreciation — calming jangled nerves, soothing lovers' brows, ensuring fidelity and devotion.

Since the days of antiquity, herbs have been present at weddings as symbols of prosperity, fertility, and love. Greek brides of long ago carried marjoram thought to promise joy; Roman brides wove sprigs of rosemary through their hair to make their marriages last. In the Middle Ages, many a wedding was blessed by brides carrying a clutch of parsley and wildflowers. Through the Elizabethan era and beyond the Victorian era, weddings were bedecked with herbal greenery in many lovely ways: in nosegays, tiny corsages, swags, sprigs tucked into the the ribbons of bride's bodice, and especially in her bouquet.

Share the wisdom and beauty of this centuries-old tradition at your celebration. Weave herbal sprigs into headpieces, tie small bouquets on chair backs, decorate doors with herbal wreaths, set tiny herb baskets by guests' plates. Their fragrance will be released, heightening the pleasure of an extraordinary day.

ROSEMARY
ensures devotion and love

SAGE
promotes good health

THYME
for courage

MARJORAM
increases marital happiness

PARSLEY
promises festive times

MINT
for strength and virtue

CHEVRIL
keeps love sincere

Heart of the Celebration

For many newly married couples, the reception dinner actually begins with cake. Amidst the laughter and tears, the dancing and speeches, somehow the courses of the meal slip by unnoticed. When it's finally time to settle down to cutting the cake, you'll want one you both love.

It's a rare bride who knows exactly what type of cake to choose. To simplify this happy task, ask to see a baker's portfolio of photographs and sample tastes from her kitchen. If you can picture in your mind's eye the cake of your dreams down to the last detail, make a sketch. Or if you have a photograph of a cake you want to replicate ⌒ perhaps your parents' very own ⌒ seek out a baker who is happy to comply.

Even though the wedding cake is meant to be eaten and enjoyed, think of it also as yet another decorative element at the reception. If the room has a lot of deep, dark color, a pale white cake stands out. A subdued room allows even a subtly colored cake to shine. At an outdoor wedding, the atmosphere calls for cakes with anything-goes touches like colorful pastillage butterflies and elaborate buttercream flowers.

To settle the delicious dilemma of frostings, as with flowers, let the season be your guide: Fall and winter are especially appropriate for cakes clad in snowy fondants and royal icing. Spring and summer cakes cannot help but tempt in buttercream, decorated with pastel tinted flowers.

Consider passing along an heirloom server to your baker for presenting the cake, or if you're lucky enough to have it, the same cake topper that crowned your parents' cakes. Don't forget the groom's cake. Today, this can be anything from the traditional fruit cake to miniature chocolate.

A Homemade
Wedding Cake

The couple who serve a homemade wedding cake enjoy the luxury of knowing how pure and delicious it will be, but it does take good planning.

- Consult baking books to calculate how much cake you will need for your guests, then design the cake. Remember to bake extra cake to save for parents and anniversaries.

- Invest in good-quality cake pans, pastry bags, and other equipment. Have a heavy-duty mixer on hand, and use the finest, freshest ingredients.

- Test for appearance, taste, and stability. Prepare a sample cake and note the timing. Bake layers that can be frozen beforehand and assembled later.

- Most wedding cakes, unless they are of temperamental whipped cream or ice cream, sit out during the reception. Check early on that the cake will not be under hot light, in sunlight, or in a busy serving area.

- Make a "test run" with your preview cake to the reception site. Wedding cakes require firm support — be sure the cake stand is sturdy.

- Create a romantic presentation for your cake, perhaps before a mirror or a decorative screen. Wrap an heirloom silver cake knife with ribbon to match the bridal bouquet, and tuck one or two non-wilting flowers inside the ribbon.

A wedding cake's look is not always determined by the kind of icing it wears. For a formal winter wedding, ornate pipings of buttercream and a topiary crown of pastillage petals create balance (left). Fondant in pale pastel brings a touch of tradition to a simple cake for a smaller wedding party (above), and stars on a marble-smooth, tiered cake that is the epitome of an informal spring wedding (opposite). The blue bows are a symbol of hope.

Interview

with a **baker**

GAIL WATSON

A Gail Watson wedding cake is a work of art, and delicious besides. This gifted baker offers her expertise to brides:

"Decide on the wedding decor first, then visit your cake maker, usually about two months before the wedding. The cake does not necessarily need to match the decor, but its color and elements need to be in keeping with the wedding theme."

"Tell your baker if an additional dessert will be served and what it will be. If it's just berries, cookies, or petit fours, you can serve a cake with a rich filling. But if heavy pastries with custard centers are on the menu, go with a lighter cake, and make it a foil for the dessert."

"Gear the filling to the season and time of day: for instance, rich chocolate cakes are wonderful in December, while light, lemony fillings are best in July. Sometimes a cake and its filling have significance to the bride and groom: for instance, we recently did a cake with a cappuccino filling, since on their first date the bride and groom had had coffee together."

"To many, buttercream is the most delicious icing, but people do shy away from it because it doesn't stand up well to heat. If you're determined, ask for a buttercream made with meringue, which stabilizes the frosting."

"Rolled fondant is pliable and allows you to achieve beautiful effects, but it cannot be refrigerated.

This really limits your choice of fillings, since many of them do need to be chilled."

"Royal icing is wonderful for piped candy flowers since it takes easily to any color and the icing dries hard. Though perhaps not as tasty as royal icing, gumpaste (also called pastillage) enables the baker to replicate the exact blooms featured in the wedding bouquet and decor."

"Also consider decorating your cake with real sugared fruits. They must be smooth skinned: grapes, kumquats, and cherries pair well with a summer wedding; in the fall, ladies apples' are lovely."

"Marzipan is a paste of ground almonds and sugar, and it is very, very rich. I never use it as an all-over icing because most people really love it or they don't like it at all. Instead, it can be shaped into life-like fruit decorations and hand-painted."

"The groom's cake is coming back into style. Traditionally, this is a rich fruitcake, but we also make them in chocolate. They can be served at the Rehearsal Dinner or at brunch the day following the wedding. We make tiny ones as wedding favors at the reception, and wrap them in little boxes for guests to take home. There is a legend that when the groom's cake is slipped under a pillow, a maid will dream of the one she will marry."

5 ROMANTIC WEDDINGS

Whether they married in a rose garden or a château, each of these couples found a romantic new way to interpret tradition. With their unique hopes and dreams very much in the foreground, they were able to work out the challenging logistics of a wedding with exceptional grace and goodwill. Their collective message: You can realize your dreams if you're willing to be flexible and imaginative.

One couple's inspiriation was to plan a wedding on Friday evening in order to secure a sought-after reception site. Another couple married in late December against the holiday lights of a big city. A spirited October bride relied on the munificence of Indian summer to marry in a

sleeveless gown at her outdoor

wedding in the woodlands. One bride and groom

stamped their reception with their new monogram. And beginning a year

ahead, the mother of a bride covered an arbor with

roses and ivy to symbolize the interfaith marriage

of her daughter and son-in-law.

What else did these couples show us? To follow

your heart: all the way to France, if you so choose,

and marry in a venerable European

tradition; or let your flower girl be two years old ⌒ as opposed

to the recommended five to seven. It's the surprise and delight of

finding your own way that unites this procession of romantic brides.

wedding
in winter

- The Lotus Club, New York City

- December 30th, 7:00 p.m.

- Black tie

- 80 guests

- Nuptial mass at St. Ignatius Loyola Catholic Church

- Table linens, placecards, menu, and groom's cake monogrammed with couple's initials

I'D ALWAYS WANTED A WINTER WEDDING," SAID KATHRYN Collins, whose romantic late December marriage to James ("Bo") still has guests reminiscing. "I'm from California and my family still lives there, so it was difficult to decide to have the wedding so far away from home. But the irresistible beauty of New York during the holidays won out."

The couple made the most of every opportunity New York offered them. They married in an after-dark service against the backdrop of the city's sparkling lights, and hosted their reception in a private club. In a stately room personalized with traditional Christmas ribbons and wreaths, intimate groupings of guests dined and danced. On that glorious evening, with candles glowing and the choir singing Beethoven's Ninth Symphony, Kathryn watched planning turn to pure magic — even snow began to fall.

"Though the wedding was formal, we wanted the reception to be very warm and friendly — more like an elegant dinner party than a banquet wedding," said Kathryn. To that end, the reception room was made intimate with small tables clustered together and personal touches — for instance, the place cards, menu cards, and napkins that Kathryn had monogrammed especially for the event with the bride's and groom's initials, a large C entwined in a K and J. "With the wide availability of machine monogramming now, it is not overly expensive to have this done," advised Kathryn. "And it is very practical: We now have what feels like a lifetime supply of linens, which we continue to use at our own dinner parties."

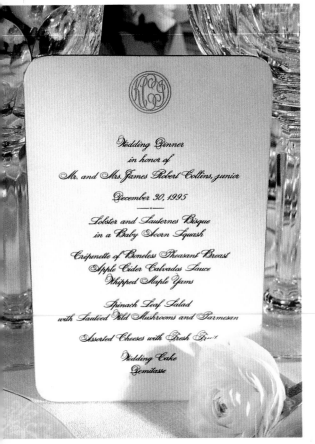

Menu card text:

*Wedding Dinner
in honor of
Mr. and Mrs. James Robert Collins, junior*

December 30, 1995

*Lobster and Sauternes Bisque
in a Baby Acorn Squash*

*Crépinette of Boneless Pheasant Breast
Apple Cider Calvados Sauce
Whipped Maple Yams*

*Spinach Leaf Salad
with Sautéed Wild Mushrooms and Parmesan*

Assorted Cheeses with Fresh Fruit

*Wedding Cake
Demitasse*

Details in winter-white echoed everywhere. A neat battalion of hand-lettered envelopes stood ready to direct guests to tables where place cards sat atop snowy napkins stitched with the couple's monogram (above). Menu cards rested against stemware (left). White gossamer ribbon fluttered on the fondant-frosted cake (opposite). As an extra fillip, each guest received a tiny groom's cake sealed with royal icing and a monogram.

wedding
in the woods

- Chapel in the woods,
  Una Estate - Soyuzivka
  Kerhonkson, New York

- October 11th, 4:00 p.m.
  Black tie

- 190 guests

- Ukranian Orthdox
  service

- Outdoor ceremony;
  seasonal fruits, flowers,
  and leaves

When Christina and Terrance Solomone planned their wedding, they knew right away where they wanted it to take place. "We first met at a New Year's party at a Ukrainian resort in the Catskill Mountains in New York, a place where my family has always had good luck for romance," remembered Christina. "At the wedding, many relatives reminded us that they had met here, too.'"

Because the rustic surroundings are always at their most beautiful in fall, the couple planned an alfresco wedding for October 11th — coincidentally the bride's birthday. "We were hoping for Indian summer, which is exactly what we got." Sunshine, gentle breezes, and gold-edged leaves graced her special day.

Since the ceremony took place in front of a chapel in a woodland clearing, guests made their ways down a meandering path to arrive at the site — with

AND MRS. RICHARD E. GILBERT

REQUEST THE HONOUR OF YOUR PRESENCE

AT THE MARRIAGE OF THEIR DAUGHTER

CHRISTINA MOTRIA

TO

PRINCE ANTHONY SOLOMON

RECEPTION
HALF AFTER FIVE O'CLOCK
SOYUZIVKA
KERHONKSON, NEW YORK

OYUZIVKA

RK

BLACK TIE

grapevine baskets of pumpkins and apples pointing the way, their colors in perfect harmony with the bride's bouquet of autumn-hued 'Leonidis' roses. For his boutonniere, the groom wore a single, perfect rose, which looked as if it could have been simply plucked from the heart of Christina's own bouquet.

"I feel so lucky to have been married at a place that has such an emotional connection for me," said Christina. "We booked the entire resort, all eighty-five rooms, and celebrated throughout the weekend: a party on Friday night, after the rehearsal dinner, and a brunch on Sunday, the day after the wedding. It made our happy occasion last a little longer."

Eggplant & Red Pepper Terrine
Tomato Basil Coulis

Beet Consommé

Caesar Salad

Filet Mignon with Sauce of Fines Herbes
Basil Mashed Potatoes
Gyoza Prawns with Sauce Crevette
Garlic Mashed Potatoes
Seasonal Spaghetti Vegetables

Creme Bruleé

Chef Andrij Sonevytsky

The bride's bouquet was designed with a just-picked look: a simple ring of full-blown burnt orange 'Leonidis' roses surrounded the center of cream-colored roses (above). Their stems were left exposed and simply cinched with a length of fine French ribbon.

Inside the reception room, seasonal touches abounded: The round tables were draped in gold brocade and had candelabra centerpieces of roses, red berries, ivy, pittosporum, and bells of Ireland (opposite). The same combination of flowers and foliage swagged the bride's seat of honor (left).

Though Christina chose a simple satin gown, she wanted more drama for her headpiece since it would be an evening reception. While in London she visited the celebrated shop of Basia Zarzycka, purveyor of enchanting one-of-a-kind accessories, where Christina found an ornate rhinestone and pearl encrusted tiara. Paired with a waterfall veil she found in the States, it twinkled magically on the dance floor. The bridesmaids wore chocolate brown velvet gowns ornamented with satin sashes, while the young flower girl, Alexandra, echoed the bride in white, complete with a demure rose bouquet of her own.

wedding
in a rose garden

"COME LIVE WITH ME, AND BE MY LOVE," SAID MATTHEW Ocken to his bride, Rachel, as they exchanged vows on a cloudless June afternoon in her parents' garden, "and I will make thee a bed of roses." So went the theme for the entire wedding, from the bride's silk taffeta dress covered with pale pink rosettes, to her bouquet of garden roses, to the rose topiaries on the tabletops at the reception — even to the garlanded arbor beneath which the two were married.

"We met as English majors in college, so we thought it was fitting to recite a Christopher Marlowe poem for our marriage," explained Rachel. Indeed, all the elements came together as if in a poem. Horses drawing the nuptial carriage pranced across the field from ceremony to reception and violinists played "Ode to Joy."

Out-of-town guests arriving for the event knew they were in the right place when they saw the box-wood heart in the center of Bridgewater, pierced with an arrow pointing the way to the wedding — the unmistakable handiwork of the bride's mother, Sue Muszala. For their daughter's wedding, the bride's parents filled their two-acre garden with special plantings of lilacs and astilbes, and they created the nuptial arbor, which served as a chuppah in the interfaith wedding. Finally, the bride's bouquet was composed of 'Oceana' roses cultivated especially to match her the silk rosettes on her gown.

To create a chuppah, the bride's mother trained roses to grow up the sides of an arbor. For the wedding day, grapevines were wrapped around the columns. Lady's mantle and 'New Dawn' roses in water-filled florists' vials (to keep them fresh) were tucked in to give the columns a lush look. As a final flourish, the chuppah was crowned with an oversize arrangement of delphiniums, Casablanca lilies, English ivy, and blue irises, all cut from the garden.

Though all of this might seem a monumental task, the elaborate prepara-tions were planned in great detail and spaced out over time, with the arbor and cutting gardens begun the year before. "It was actually much easier than renting a catering hall," Mrs. Muszala reflected later. "This way, we knew that every detail would be perfect."

"We had that bed of roses from the Marlowe poem — well, it was a path, really," recalled Rachel. Because the skirt of her gown was too wide for the garden's real path, a "wedding aisle" was created with pastel-toned rose petals, some from the garden, others from friends' gardens, and still others donated by a local florist. When the bride walked down the fragrant aisle to join her groom, it was an especially moving moment for everyone present.

As a rabbi and a minister presided, the newlyweds sealed their vows by drinking from a wedding cup — the same one that the bride's parents had shared on their own wedding day.

wedding
in a mansion

- James Burden Mansion, New York City

- July 25th, 5:30 p.m.

- Black tie optional

- 110 guests

- Chapel of an Episcopalian church

- Dotted Swiss theme for fabrics, wedding cake, and desserts

I NEVER PICTURED MYSELF WALKING ALONG THE STREETS OF Manhattan in a bridal gown," laughed Katie Nelson, fondly recalling her wedding to John, which took place early one balmy July evening. "But the reception and church were only a block apart, so the thing to do was to get there on foot — which was also so convenient for the guests."

To make matters more unusual, the couple held their nuptials on a Friday: "The reception room that we had our hearts set on was reserved for Saturdays and Sundays a year in advance. But John and I really didn't want to wait. We thought — why not a Friday evening? Many of our guests would be leaving work then and be ready to have a good time. Since the ceremony was held late in the afternoon, we wanted to encourage lots of dancing. Our reception had the feeling of a great party."

As a six-piece orchestra played favorites from the couple's college years, guests entered the ballroom of the mansion to find tables shimmering with pale green floral brocade cloths — a garden color that beautifully offset centerpiece arrangements in pedestal vases (opposite). To enhance the breezy summery theme, each fold-up chair wore an awning stripe slipcover (above). The bride's seat of honor was accented with a tieback of pale roses with fabric that matched both her bouquet and the bow on the back of her gown (right).

When Katie was working with the baker to come up with a cake design as intriguing as the table settings, her eye suddenly rested on a swatch of the dotted Swiss fabric that was to be used for the napkins. "We agreed that it is was the perfect white-on-white pattern for fondant icing." To the guests' delight, the cake table displayed a dotted Swiss cake garlanded with pastry roses. Matching fondant-iced cookie hearts presented in silver baskets were another tempting dessert. "For the wedding favors, we offered small decorative pillows. The top of each was embroidered with the same fleur-de-lys pattern found on the chapel walls of the church. It was a symbolic way of joining the ceremony to the reception."

On that magical summer evening, the entire bridal party was turned out to tailored perfection. Katie wore an elegant peau de soie satin gown paired with a classic pillbox hat and veil, while the groom donned formal white tie and tails. "I think the wedding was even more special to my family because my nieces and nephew participated," said Katie. Acting as a junior bridesmaid, Katie Lynn, thirteen, wore a floor-length navy blue dress with cap sleeves (a more demure version of the maid of honor's evening gown), while six-year-old Kelly was a charming flower girl in a swirl of white silk and organdy, with three-year-old Gregory as ringbearer. In a meaningful bow to the past, Katie carried a prayer book that had been inscribed by generations of brides in her family, destined to be passed along to her attendants and generations to come.

wedding
at a château

❤ 17th-century family
château, Brittany, France

❤ July 29th, 3:30 p.m.

❤ Full dress

❤ 450 guests

❤ Catholic nuptial mass

❤ The countryside in full
hydrangea bloom; the
entire village in attendance

ON THE WEDDING DAY OF ELIZABETH MORAN TO SEBASTIEN
de Longeaux, not only did all of the groom's family turn out to shower the
couple with rose petals, but an entire French town besides. "Here the church
doors must remain open to all ⟶ it's good luck," said the American-born
bride, who met her future husband while she was a student in Paris.

Knowing that the church was designed by the groom's great-great uncle,
Elizabeth found her eye straying to the architectural details during the ceremony. She discovered one that was particularly touching: "In the stained glass
was a picture of the château owned by Sebastien's family where we would be
having our reception. It had been placed there by the architect to honor his
ancestral home. I kept thinking of all the de Longeaux brides before me who
had also admired it on their wedding days."

Dressed in chic hats and wedding finery, the whole village turned out to celebrate at the de Longeaux château. The wedding was truly a family affair; for example, Sebastien's sister helped Elizabeth find her embroidered silk gown and made the flowergirl dresses herself. The French custom is that all the attendants are children, in this case, the groom's nieces and nephews. Though the event was steeped in French tradition, there was a distinctly American touch: Both of Elizabeth's parents walked her down the aisle.

While the reception took place at the groom's family château, Elizabeth's family also played a role. Her two sisters acted as witnesses at the civil ceremony, performed by the town mayor. Sebastien's brother, a priest, presided over the nuptial mass that preceded the late-afternoon reception.

"We left the reception rooms open in the château just in case of rain, but it turned out to be a gorgeous day and everyone dined under tents outdoors," said Elizabeth. "The food was simple and classic: foie gras, local cheeses, fish cooked in the regional style, served with white wine and Champagne, followed by an iced dessert. Guests had come from all over Europe and America, but there didn't seem to be any language barrier, especially when it came to dancing. Unlike in America, where there is a set guest list, here everyone is invited. It is a chance for a grand reunion of family and friends."

Dating from the 17th century, the stone château provided a breathtaking background. "Fortunately for us, it was available whenever we needed it, since it is in the de Longeaux family," said Elizabeth. "We chose late July for the wedding because we knew the hydrangeas would be at their peak."

Many other customs at the reception held interesting contrasts for the bride. "In France, people don't really give toasts so much as speeches. Friends spend days preparing them, so the reception was quite touching, filled with good will and humor. There is even a traditional game that the bride and groom have to play: Sebastien and I sat in two chairs placed back to back while we were asked questions about each other's likes and dislikes, without the benefit of watching each other's expression — it's a way of couples getting to know one another better before they begin married life."

The reception was such a success the newlyweds stayed on and on.

"I researched the countryside of Brittany for special touches that would help to make our wedding memorable, and came across a museum of Americana, of all things, run by a local collector," recalled Elizabeth. *"When he found out that I was from the United States he was more than delighted to lend us a pristine, vintage Park Lewis car, which we used to get from the church to the reception."*

"Sebastien and I left at 3 o'clock in the morning, but the party continued until dawn. Then later in the day, many guests returned to the château, where they were treated to the traditional post-wedding feast of crêpes and cider."

Credits

CONTRIBUTORS

CONTRIBUTORS

PHOTOGRAPHY

jacket image by Steve Ladner

1	Toshi Otsuki		50	top, Thomas Hooper
2-11	Toshi Otsuki			bottom, Luciana Pampalone
15	Theo Gruttman		51	top left, Toshi Otsuki
16	Toshi Otsuki			bottom left, Luciana Pampalone
17	top, Jana Taylor			top right, Toshi Otsuki
	bottom, Cyndy Warwick		51	bottom right, Luciana Pampalone
18	Wendi Schneider		52	Toshi Otsuki
19	top, Toshi Otsuki		53	Nadia Rein
19	bottom, Carlos Spaventa		55-57	Thomas Hooper
20	Toshi Otsuki		59	Carin Krasner
	left, Guy Bouchet		60	left, Wendi Schneider
	right, Jana Taylor		60	right, Toshi Otsuki
23	top, Toshi Otsuki		62	Jana Taylor
	bottom, Starr Ockenga		63	Cyndy Warwick
	right, Luciana Pampalone		64-65	Luciana Pampalone
24-25	Toshi Otsuki		66	Thomas Hooper
26	William P. Steele		67	Toshi Otsuki
27	Guy Bouchet		69	Steve Gross
28	Michael Skott		70	Luciana Pampalone
29	Toshi Otsuki		71	Toshi Otsuki
31	Luciana Pampalone		72	Wendi Schneider
32	Toshi Otsuki		73	Susanna Brown
34	Steve Ladner		74	Thomas Hooper
35-36	Luciana Pampalone		75	left, Toshi Otsuki
37	Guy Bouchet			right, Michael Skott
39	Steven Randazzo		76-77	Wendi Schneider
40	Starr Ockenga		78	top, Luciana Pampalone
41	Luciana Pampalone			bottom, Toshi Otsuki
42	Wendi Schneider		79-81	Toshi Otsuki
45	Mallory Samson		82	Jana Taylor
46	Toshi Otsuki		84	Elyse Lewin
47	Jana Taylor		85	Jana Taylor
48-49	Toshi Otsuki		86	top, Toshi Otsuki
50	left, Luciana Pampalone			bottom, Michael Skott
			87-88	Toshi Otsuki
			89	Theo Gruttman

PHOTOGRAPHY

Best

Sources

CONTENTS

VICTORIA
OUR PRIVATE
COLLECTION
(800) 223-3089
**Exclusive designs for fashion
and celebration**

BEAUTY

BLISS SPA
(212) 219-8970
568 Broadway
New York, NY 10012
**Body treatments, skin care and
facials; manicures**

BROWNES & CO.
APOTHECARY
(305) 532-8784
(888)-BROWNES
841 Lincoln Rd.
Miami Beach, FL 33139
**Natural skin-care supplies and
salon. Catalog**

CHARLES IFERGAN
(312) 642-4484
106 East Oak St.
Chicago, IL 60611
Hair salon and makeup

C.O. BIGELOW
CHEMISTS
(212) 473-7324
414 Avenue of the Americas
New York, NY 10011
**Natural skin-care products.
Catalog**

COLOURS SALON
(206) 284-6041
2409 Queen Anne Ave. N.
Seattle, WA
Hair salon

ETTIE ELJAMAL
(212) 460-8500
New York, NY
**Electrolysis, waxing, brow
shaping; by appointment**

FRESH
(617) 421-1212
121 Newbury St.
Boston, MA 02116
Fragrances, skin care

GUI VRABL
(212) 316-5727
New York, NY
Beauty expert

JOLIE THE DAY SPA
(404) 266-0060
3619 Piedmont Rd.
Atlanta, GA 30305

KIEHL'S PHARMACY
(800) KIEHLS-1
109 3rd Ave.
New York, NY 10003
**Hair and skin-care products,
cosmetics. Catalog**

MAKEUP CENTER
(212) 977-9494
150 W. 55th St.
New York, NY 10019
**Make-overs and cosmetics; by
appointment**

MARIA RUSSO SALON
(617) 424-6676
9 Newbury St.
Boston, MA 02116
Full-service salon

MARIANA'S SKIN CARE
(978) 922-0707
498 Elliot St.
Beverly, MA 01915
Makeup, facials, body treatments

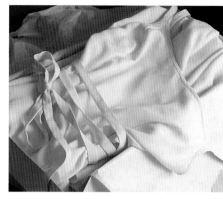

Hamilton Kennedy

THE MARILYN MIGLIN
INSTITUTE
(800) 662-1120
112 East Oak St.
Chicago, IL 60611
Cosmetics, skincare and fragrance

MINARDI SALON
(212) 308-1711
29 E. 61st St., 5th Fl.
New York, NY 10021
Hair color

PETER ANTHONY
STUDIO
(801) 649-9595
Park City, UT
Full-service salon

THE PHOENIX SALON
(214) 352-8411
5600 West Lovers Lane
Dallas, TX 75209
Hair styling and cosmetics

RONNI KOLOTKIN
(212) 366-6663
New York, NY
**Electrolysis, brow shaping, by
appointment**

SALON CRISTOPHE
(202) 785-2222
1125 18th St.
Washington, DC
Hair salon, makeup consultants

SALLY BEAUTY
SUPPLIES
(214) 720-1910
(800) 284-7255
Dallas, TX
**Cosmetics and beauty supplies.
Catalog**

SCENTIMENTS
& ESSENTIALS AT
FRED SEGAL
(310) 394-8509
500 Broadway
Santa Monica, CA 90401
Natural beauty products

SKIN CARE FOR THE
NINETIES
(415) 285-4868
San Francisco, CA
Makeup and skin care

STRAWBERRY JAM
(215) 862-9251
44C South Main
New Hope, PA 18938
Aromatherapy, natural products

SUE FISHER KING
(415) 922-7276
3067 Sacramento St.
San Francisco, CA 94115
Toiletries

SUSAN CIMINELLI
DAY SPA
(212) 872-2650
Bergdorf Goodman
New York, NY
Skin care, massages, spa treatments

SYLVIE'S
(818) 905-8815
17071 Ventura Blvd.
Encino, CA 91316
Skin-care salon, manicures

The Bearlace Cottage

TONI & GUY
(214) 696-3825
6030 Sherry Lane
Dallas, TX 75225
Hairstyling and makeup

A TOUCH OF IVY
(609) 252-1191
203-205 Witherspoon St.
Princeton, NJ 08542
Original fragrances and gifts

VALERIE
BEVERLY HILLS
(800) 282-5374
460 N. Cannon
Beverly Hills, CA 90210
Makeup lessons, cosmetics, by appointment only

YOSHI FOR HAIR
(415) 989-7704
173 Maiden Lane
San Francisco, CA 94108
Consultation required

FASHION

ALBERTA FERRETTI
Bloomingdale's, NY;
Dillards, TX; and Nordstrom, CA
Custom gowns

ALENÇON
(415) 389-9408
318 Miller Ave.
Mill Valley, CA 94941
Custom gowns, veils, and head-pieces

AMANDA MAY
DESIGNS
(204) 727-4962
RR3, Box 103, Suite 30
Brandon, Manitoba, R7A 5Y3
Canada
Gowns

AMAZON DRY GOODS
(319) 322-6800 or (800) 798-7979
2218 E. 11th St.
Davenport, IA 52803
Victorian fashions, accessories, patterns, shoes. Catalog

AMIANA
at Shoofly. New York
(212)580-4390
and Pixie Town, Los Angeles
(213) 272-6415
Flower girl shoes

AMSALE
(212) 971-0170
(800) 765-0170
New York, NY
Call for local availability

AMY DOWNS
(212) 598-4189
New York, NY
Custom hats

AMY JO GLADSTONE
(718) 899-8010
Long Island City, NY
Custom work, boudoir slippers, silk creations

ANDERE LINGERIE
(913) 677-3803
Topeka, KS

ANGEL SANCHEZ
(323) 921-9287
Call for local availability

ANGÈLE PARLANGE
DESIGN
(504) 897-6511
5419 Magazine Street
New Orleans, LA 70115
Silk bridal purses

ANITA PAGLIARO, LTD.
(212) 737-2684
1030 Lexington Ave.
New York, NY 10021
Bridal gowns

ANN LAWRENCE
ANTIQUES
(505) 982-1755
369 Montezuma #210
Santa Fe, NM 87501
Antique gowns

ANN VUILLE
(212) 826-8900
at Barneys, New York
Headbands

ARICIE LINGERIE
DE MARQUE
(415) 989-0261
50 Post St.
San Francisco, CA 94104

ARLOTTA
(212) 779-0711
New York, NY
**Foundations and corsetry.
Call for local availability**

BADGLEY MISCHKA
(212) 921-1585
New York, NY
Call for local availability

BASIA ZARZYCKA
(011) 44-171-351-7276
135 Kings Road
London, England SW3 4PW
Custom gowns, corsetry, and shoes

BÊBÊ THOMPSON
(212) 249-4740
1216 Lexington Ave.
New York, NY 10028
Flower girl fashions

BETTINA
(415) 563-8002
3654 Sacramento St.
San Francisco, CA 94118

THE BEARLACE
COTTAGE
(801) 649-8804
PO Box 702
412 Marsac
Park City, UT 84060
Hard-to-find heirloom laces and antique gowns

BELLA DONNA
(415) 861-7182
539 Hayes St.
San Francisco, CA 94102
Custom gowns, veils, and shoes

BIRNBAUM & BULLOCK
(212) 242-2914
New York, NY
Custom gowns

BOB EVANS
(212) 889-1999
New York, NY
Custom gowns; call for local availability

BOWDON DESIGNER
FASHION
(707) 525.8054
838 Fourth St.
Santa Rosa, CA 95404

BRAVO BRAS
(800) 55-BRAVO
7200 France Ave. South. #331
Edina, MN 55435
Custom corsetry, by appointment only

BRUNI NIGH
(415) 346-3299
2384 Union St.
San Francisco, CA 94122
Custom headwear and accessories

CAPEZIO DANCE
THEATRE SHOP
(212) 245-2130
1650 Broadway
New York, NY 10019
Ballet slippers. Catalog

CAROLINA AMATO
(212) 768-9095
(800) GLOVE-95
New York, NY
Gloves

CAROLINA HERRERA
(212) 944-5757
501 Seventh Ave.
New York, NY 10018
Custom gowns; call for local availability

CARRIE FORBES
(310) 448-1788
Los Angeles, CA
Crochet evening bags

CATHERINE BUCKLEY
(011) 44-171-229-1028
116 Kensington Park Rd.
London W11 2PW England
By appointment

CESAR GALINDO
(310) 392-3911
at Framm
2667 Main St.
Santa Monica, CA 90405
Vintage and custom gowns

CHALLONER, NYC
(212) 274-1437
New York, NY
Headpieces, gloves, handbags

CHAPEAUX CARINE
(212) 777-8393
New York, NY
Custom hat designs

CHRISTIAN DIOR
(800) 341-3467
Call for local availability

CHRISTINA KARA
(212) 228-7744
125 St. Marks Place
New York, NY 10009
and (212) 579-2089
310 Columbus Ave.
New York, NY 10023
Custom veils and gowns

CHRISTOPHER HUNTE
(212) 244-0420
New York, NY
Custom gowns

THE COBBLESTONE
ROSE
(313) 944-6202
Saline, Michigan
Veils and headpieces

CORNELIA POWELL
(404) 365-8511
271 E. Paces Ferry Rd.
Atlanta, GA 30305
Antique lace gowns, veils, headpieces, shoes

COUP DE CHAPEAUX
(415) 931-7793
1821 Steiner
San Francisco, CA
Original and vintage designs, millinery restoration

CREATIONS
FRANÇOISE
BOUTHILLIER
at Jones & Jones
(210) 687-1171
Dresses and coats

CYNTHIA ROWLEY
(212) 334-1144
112 Wooster St.
New York, NY 10011
and (773) 528-6160
808 West Armitage
Chicago, IL 60614
Formal wear and shoes

DARBY SCOTT
(212) 874-0201
New York, NY
Dresses by special order

DIANE HAMELINE
(011) 331-42-78-57-32
85 Rue Wiellle D Temple
75003 Paris, France

DONALD DEAL
at Bergdorf Goodman Bridal
(212) 872-8957
Bridal gowns

DONNA KARAN
(800) 647-7474
New York, NY
Call for local availability.

ELISA CASAS
(800) 331-1909
63 Thompson St.
New York, NY 10002
Custom gowns

EMMA HOPE'S SHOES
(011) 44-171-833-2367
33 Amwell St.
London EC1 1UR England
and (011) 44-171-259-9566
12 Symons St., London
Shoes

ENDRIUS
(212) 838-5880
New York, NY
Couture gowns

ERICA TANOV
(510) 524-1762
1627 San Pablo Ave.
Berkeley, CA 94702
Lingerie

ERIC JAVITS
(800) 374-HATS
Veils and pillbox hats

EXCLUSIVES
FOR THE BRIDE
(312) 664-8870
Chicago, IL

FINO FINO
(415) 321-8720
Allied Arts Guild
75 Arbor Road
Menlo Park, CA 94025
Custom veils

FORGET ME KNOTS
(415) 921-0838
1738 Union St.
San Francisco, CA 94123
Bridesmaid dresses, bridal accessories and wedding favors

GENE LONDON
(212) 533-4105
(212) 929-3349
New York, NY
Accessories and gowns

GENTLE ARTS
(504) 895-5628
4500 Dryads St., Ste. B
New Orleans, LA 70115
Textile restoration specializing in lace

GILLIAN SWONNELL
(617) 542-3242
535 Albany St.
Boston, MA 02118
Contemporary gowns

GINA BIANCO
(212) 924-1685
New York, NY
Textile and gown conservation and restorations, custom headpieces

GIORDANO'S
(212) 688-7195
1150 2nd Ave.
New York, NY 10021
Shoes in sizes 4 to 6 only. Catalog

HANG FEN
(212) 695-9509
New York, NY
Gowns, shawls, handbags

Belle Meline

HAMILTON KENNEDY
at Takashimaya
(212) 350-0100
693 Fifth Ave.
New York, NY 10022
Lingerie

THE HAT SHOP
(212) 219-1445
120 Thompson St.
New York, NY 10012

HELEN KIRKWOOD
(011) 44-780-57141
14 St. Mary's Street
Stamford, Lincolnshire PE9 2DF
England
Custom gowns

HELEN MORLEY
(212) 594-6404
New York, NY
Call for local availability

HELENE ARPELS
(212) 755-1623
470 Park Ave.
New York, NY 10021
Dress shoes, evening slippers, accessories

HENRI BENDEL
(212) 247-1100
712 Fifth Ave.
New York, NY 10019
Department store

HERITAGE WEDDING
GOWN COLLECTION
at the Amherst Museum
(716) 689-1440
Colony Park
3755 Tonawanda Creek Rd.
East Amherst, NY 14051
Vintage gowns collection; call for information

HERSCHELLE
COUTURIER
(415) 982-0112
San Francisco, CA
Custom formal wear and gowns

H.M. WOGGLEBUG
(401) 751-7787
350 South Main St.
Providence, RI 02903
Children's dresses

HOLLY WILSON
SAUNDERS
(708) 386-8806
54 W. Washington
Oak Park, IL 60302
Custom wedding gowns and restoration

HOMA
(201) 655-1239
Montclair, NJ
Veils, bridal accessories

IMPRESSIONS
(404) 841-6202
Atlanta, GA
Bridal gowns, veils, accessories

ISAAC MIZRAHI
(800) 340-6004
New York, NY
Call for local availability

JANA STARR ANTIQUES
(212) 861-8256
236 E. 80th St.
New York, NY 10021
Refitting Edwardian fashions, accessories

JANE WILSON
(212) 477-4408
155 Prince St., lower level
New York, NY 10012
Bridal gowns, veils, headpieces; mother-of-the-bride and flower girl fashions

JEAN HOFFMAN
ANTIQUES
(212) 535-6930
207 E. 66th St.
New York, NY 10021
Antique gowns, lace, accessories. Restoration services

JEANNIE'S FANTASIA
(615) 352-1726
611 Hillwood Blvd.
Nashville, TN 37205
Reproductions of antique gowns and headpieces

JESSICA MCCLINTOCK
(800) 333-5301
(310) 273-9690
9517 Wilshire Blvd.
Beverly Hills, CA 90210
Call for local availability

JLM COUTURE
(212) 921-7058
New York, NY
Gowns

JOAN CALABRESE
(503) 538-1576
Riverside Drive N.E.
St. Paul, OR 97137
Flower girl dresses

JOAN GILBERT BRIDAL
COLLECTION
(415) 752-2456
San Francisco, CA
Veils, by appointment

JOHN ANTHONY
SALON
(212) 888-4070
153 E. 61st St.
New York, NY 10021
Gowns, shawls

KAREN AUGUSTA
ANTIQUE LACE AND
FASHION
(802) 463-4958
Westminster, VT
Call for local availability

KATHRYN NIXON
(212) 979-8699
New York, NY
Custom dressmaker

KEEPSAKE DESIGNS BY
CECILIA HARDIN
(502) 459-7160
Louisville, KY

KEVIN SIMON
CLOTHING
(310) 392-4630
1358 Abbot Kinney Blvd.
Venice, CA 90291
Custom wedding gowns; by appointment

LA CRASIA
(212) 594-2223
304 Fifth Ave.
New York, NY 10001
Custom gloves

LAKU
(415) 695-1462
1069 Valencia
San Francisco, CA 94110
Gowns, veils, accessories, and shoes

LA PERLA
(212) 570.0050
777 Madison Ave.
New York, NY 10011
Silk foundations; call for local availability

LAURIE BELL
(336) 370-9503
805 W. McGee St.
Greensboro, NC 27401
Lace blouses and vests

LEGACY
(212) 966-4827
109 Thompson St.
New York, NY 10012
Headpieces, veils, and gowns

LES HABITUDES
(310) 273-2883
101 N. Robertson Blvd.
Los Angeles, CA 90048
Gowns

LINDA DRESNER
(212) 308-3177
484 Park Ave.
New York, NY 10022
and (248) 642-4999
299 West Maple Rd.
Birmingham, MI 48009
Custom gowns

LISA HAMMERQUIST
(518) 434-9151
Albany, NY
Dresses; by appointment

LISA SHAUB
(212) 675-9701
615 Hudson St.
New York, NY 10014
Custom millinery and veils

LILY
(310) 724-5757
9044 Burton Way
Beverly Hills, CA 90211
Vintage gowns and lingerie

LOLA MILLINERY
at Bergdorf Goodman
(212) 753-7500
Hats

MAJOLIE ATELIER
(215) 483-8850
Philadelphia, PA

MANAL
(212) 760-0121
212 W. 35th St.
New York, NY 10001
Gowns; by appointment

MARIA JUNG
COUTURIER
(305) 461-2090
370 Miracle Mile
Coral Gables, FL 33134
**Custom gowns and accessories
for attendants**

MARK CALIGIURI
(612) 339-5772
Minneapolis, MN 55403
Couture gowns

MARY ADAMS
(212) 473-0237
159 Ludlow St.
New York, NY 10002
Custom contemporary gowns

MARY ELLEN &
COMPANY
(219) 656-3000
(800) 669-1860
100 N. Main St.
North Liberty, IN 46554
**Victorian reproductions and
theme weddings. Catalog**

MARY FREDERICKSON
(806) 655-1362
1420 4th Ave., Ste. 22
Canyon, TX 79015
Restoration

MARY JANE DENZER
(914) 328-0330
222 Mamaroneck Avenue
White Plains, NY 10605
Mother-of-the-bride gowns only

MEG COHEN DESIGN
(212) 473-4002
New York, NY
**Silk chiffon stoles, cashmere
scarves**

MILLTEX
(212) 779-4366
New York, NY
**Poupie Cardolle corsets; call for
local availability**

MILO
(214) 522-1118
4337 Lovers Lane
Dallas, TX 75225
Custom dresses

MORGANE LE FAY
(212) 879-9700
746 Madison Ave.
New York, NY 10021
Gowns

MORRISON, MARINA
(415) 781-7920
San Francisco, CA
**Gowns, veils, headpieces, jewelry,
shoes, bridal party attire**

MUSEUM QUALITY
PRESERVATION
(800) 937-2693 or (914) 769-4956
9 Laurel Lane
Pleasantville, NY 10570
**Conservation and cleaning of
gowns**

NANCY ANGEL OF
ANGEL THREADS
(212) 673-4592
151 First Avenue, Box 159
New York, NY 10003
**Bridal accessories and linens by
mail. Catalog**

NANCY BACICH
(212) 673-6068
New York, NY
Gloves and handbags

NANCY MEYER FINE
LINGERIE
(206) 625-9200
1318 Fifth Ave.
Seattle, WA 98101

NEEVEGAYLE
(888) 224-2224
**Sea Island cotton; call for local
availability**

NORMA KAMALI
(212) 957-9797
11 West 56th St.
New York, NY 10019
Call for local availability

OUT OF THE PAST
(718) 748-1490
9012 3rd Ave.
Brooklyn, NY 11209
Antique fashions and accessories

PAMELA DENNIS
(212) 354-2100
New York, NY
Gowns

PANTAGES
(206) 528-1922
2655 NE University Village
Seattle, WA 98105
Lingerie

PARIS 1900
(310) 396-0405
2703 Main Street
Santa Monica, CA 90405
Antique and restored gowns

PAT KERR
(901) 525-5223
Memphis, TN
**Heirloom lace gown designs and
children's fashions; call for local
availability**

PATRICIA GOURLAY
(203) 869-0977
45 East Putnam Rd.
Greenwich, CT 06830
Lingerie

PATRICIA
UNDERWOOD
(212) 268.3774
New York, NY
**Hats in straw, felt, fur; call for
local availability**

PHILLIPE MODEL
(011) 33-42-96-8902
33 Place du Marche
Saint-Honore, Paris 75001
France
Shoes

PETER FOX SHOES
(212) 431-7426
105 Thompson St.
New York, NY
Shoes. Catalog

PO COUTURE
(212) 921-0049
New York, NY
Gowns and veils

POSIE'S
(207) 236-0000
519 West St.
Rockport, ME 04856
Children's fashions

PRISCILLA OF BOSTON
(617) 267-9070
137 Newbury St.
Boston, MA 02116
Gowns, headpieces, shoes; call for local availability

PROVERBS 31 (PEGGY OLOUMI & CATHY JOHNSTON)
(800) 655-4349
9114 Adams Ave., Suite 144
Huntington Beach, CA 92646
Antique and reproduction accessories, veils, pillows

RALPH LAUREN
(212) 642-8700
New York, NY

REEM ACRA/REEM BRIDALS
(212) 431-9232
New York, NY
Custom gowns and accessories

REVIVALS
at Metropolitan Design Group
Bergdorf Goodman, New York
(212) 753-7300

RICHARD BROOKS COUTURE FABRICS
(214) 739-2772
6131 Luther Lane Suite 200
Dallas, TX 75225
Custom gowns

RICHARD GLASGOW
(212) 683-1300
New York, NY
Gowns; call for local availability

RICHARD TYLER
(213) 931-9678
7290 Beverly Blvd.
Los Angeles, CA 90036
Custom bridal gowns

ROBERT CLERGERIE
at Barneys New York
(212) 826-8900
Shoes

ROBERT DANES
(212) 941-5680
New York, NY
Bridal specialists

RODNEY TELFORD
(212) 334-4676
89 Grand St.
New York, NY 10013
Attendants' gowns

SANDRA JOHNSON COUTURE
(310) 247-8206
138 S. Robertson Blvd.
Los Angeles, CA
Gowns

SERAFINA
(212) 253-2754
29 E. 19th St.
New York, NY 10003
Custom attendants' gowns

SEWTIQUE
(860) 445-7320
391 Long Hill Rd.
Groton, CT 06340
Wedding gown restorer

SHANEEN HUXHAM
(212) 944-6110
New York, NY
Handmade gloves; call for local availability

SIGERSON MORRISON
(212) 219-3893
242 Mott St.
New York, NY 10012
Shoes

SILK, SATIN AND LACE
(415) 435-1237
13 Main St.
Tiburon, CA 94920
Lingerie

SOPP
(800) 233-2697
Hair ribbons

SOUTHERN HEIRLOOMS BY EDIE JORDAN
(601) 289-1815
305 N. Natchez Suite G
Kosciusko, MS 39090
Veils

SPOSABELLA LACE
(212) 354-4729
252 W. 40th St.
New York, NY 10018
Fabrics, custom millinery, dressmaking

STACCATO
(415) 381-1746
30 Miller Ave.
Mill Valley, CA 94941
Veils

STÉPHANIE LESAINT HAUTE COUTURE
(201) 792-0208
Hoboken, NJ
Bridal gowns; by appointment

STRASBURG, INC. AT VELVETEEN RABBIT
(601) 844-1678
Flower girl dresses

STUART WEITZMAN
(212) 582-9500
New York, NY
Shoes; call for local availability

STUBBS & WOOTEN
(212) 249-5200
22 East 72nd St.
New York, NY 10021
Custom bridal for men and women; boudoir slippers

SUE EKAHN
(212) 929-4432
New York, NY
Custom lingerie; call for local availability

SUZANNE SPELLAN
(718) 789-4476
Brooklyn, NY
Custom dressmaker

SWEET PEAS
(718) 680-5766
8416 3rd Avenue
Brooklyn, NY 11209
Flower girl dresses

SYDNEY BUSH
(212) 563-8023
New York, NY
Traditional bridal lingerie; call for local availability

THOMASINA
(412) 563-7788
615 Washington Rd.
Mt. Lebanon, PA 15228
Custom gowns

TIA MAZZA
(212) 989-4349
New York, NY
Handmade crowns and veils; call for local availability

TIME AFTER TIME
(213) 653-8463
7425 Melrose Ave.
Los Angeles, CA 90046
Vintage bridal fashions

TOUJOURS
(415) 346-3988
2484 Sacramento St.
San Francisco, CA 94115
Bridal lingerie, hosiery, and accessories

TROUVAILLE FRANÇAISE
(212) 737-6015
New York, NY
Victorian fashions, petticoats, linens, laces

ULLA-MAIJA
(212) 570-6085
New York, NY
Couture gowns; call for local availability

VERA WANG
(212) 628-3400
991 Madison Ave.
New York, NY 10023
Custom bridal gowns, veils, accessories

VERENA DESIGNS
(336) 869-8235
High Point, NC
Lingerie; call for local availability

VIVIAN NICOLE
(718) 812-8130
New York, NY
Children's fashions; call for local availability

WEARKSTATT
(212) 334-9494
33 Greene St.
New York, NY 10013
Custom gowns

J. M. WESTON
(212) 308-5655
42 East 57th St.
New York, NY 10022
Men's shoes

YUMI KATSURA
(212) 772-3760
907 Madison Ave.
New York, NY 10021
Gowns; by appointment

ZAZU & VIOLETS
(510) 845-1409
1790 Shattuck Ave.
Berkeley, CA 94709
Bridal shoes, accessories, custom headpieces

FABRICS & TRIMMINGS

B & J FABRICS, INC
(212) 354-8150
263 West 40th St.
New York, NY 10018
Silks, embroidery, chantilly lace

BELL'OCCHIO
(415) 864-4048
8 Brady St.
San Francisco, CA 94103
Vintage ribbons, silk roses, unusual accessories.

BRITEX FABRICS
(415) 392-2910
146 Geary St.
San Francisco, CA 94108
Vintage buttons

CINDERELLA
(212) 840-0644
60 W. 38th St.
New York, NY 10018
Ribbons, trimmings, silk flowers. Catalog

DIAMOND
(213) 931-8148
611 S. La Brea Ave.
Los Angeles, CA 90036

FABRIC CENTER
(978) 343-4402
485 Electric Avenue
Fitchburg, MA 01420

FIONA BARCLAY
9 Mt. Pleasant
Keyworth,
Nottinghamshire NG12 5EP
England

GARDNER'S RIBBONS & LACE
(817) 640-1436
2235 E. Division
Arlington, TX 76011
Vintage lace, buttons, beads, and trims

HEAVEN ON LA BREA
(213) 965-8200
612 South La Brea
Los Angeles, CA
Vintage fabrics, trimmings, and lace

HYMAN HENDLER & SONS
(212) 840-8393
67 West 38th. St.
New York, NY 10018
Vintage ribbons

INTERNATIONAL SILKS & WOOLENS
(213) 653-6453
8347 Beverly Blvd.
Los Angeles, CA 90048

LACIS
(510) 843-7290
2982 Adeline St.
Berkeley, CA 94073
Lace

LOOSE ENDS
(503) 390-7457
3824 River Rd.
North Kaizer, OR 97303
Ribbons, papers. Catalog

M & J TRIMMING
(212) 391-9072
1008 Ave. of the Americas
New York, NY 10028
Custom millinery, notions, trimmings, and buttons

MIDORI, INC.
(206) 282-3595
3524 West Government Way
Seattle, WA 98199
Ribbons; call for local availability

MON COEUR BY JANET
BRUNO-SMALL
(504) 488-4775
422 S. Clark
New Orleans, LA 70119

MOSKATEL'S
(213) 689-4830
738 S. Wall St.
Los Angeles, CA 90014

POPPY FABRICS
(510) 655-5151
5151 Broadway
Oakland, CA 94611

PROMENADE FABRICS
(504) 522-1488
1520 St. Charles Ave.
New Orleans, LA 70130
Ribbons and fabrics

REFLECTIONS OF
THE PAST
P.O. Box 40361
Bay Village, OH 44140

THE RIBBONRY
(419) 872-0073
119 Louisiana Ave.
Perrysburg, OH 43551
Ribbons. Catalog

RICHARD BROOKS
COUTURE FABRICS
(214) 739-2772
6131 Luther Lane, Suite 200
Dallas, TX 75226

SCHUMACHER
(800) 332-3384
Call for local availability

SEWTIQUE
(860) 445-7320
391 Long Hill Rd.
Groton, CT 06340
Antique fabrics

SLIPS
(415) 362-5652
1534 Grant Ave.
San Francisco, CA 94133
**Slipcovers for bride's chair,
linens; custom work**

SPOSABELLA LACE
(212) 354-4729
252 W. 40th St.
New York, NY 10018
Fabrics and trimming

TAIL OF THE YAK
(510) 841-9891
2632 Ashby Ave.
Berkeley, CA 94705

TENDER BUTTONS
(212) 758-7004
143 E. 62nd
New York, NY 10021
and (312) 337-7033
946 North Rush Street
Chicago, IL 60611

TINSEL TRADING
COMPANY
(212) 730-1030
47 West 38th St.
New York, NY 10018
Vintage flowers and metallics

A TOUCH OF IVY
(609) 252-1191
203-205 Witherspoon St.
Princeton, NJ 08542
Ribbons, fabrics

VABAN
(800) 822-2606
Ribbons

V V ROULEAUX
(011) 44-171-730-3125
10 Simons St.
Sloane Square SW3 2TJ
London, England
**Ribbon, trimmings, braids.
Catalog**

WAVERLY
(800) 423-5881
Fabrics; call for local availability

WHITCHURCH SILK
MILL
28 Wincester St.
Whitchurch, Hampshire
RG28 7AL England

WOLFE, MARGARET
(310) 322-1397
Los Angeles, CA
**Victorian ribbonwork; by
appointment**

ANGELA CUMMINGS
BOUTIQUE
(212) 872-8874
754 Fifth Ave.
New York, NY 10019
Wedding bands and jewelry

BRENDA SCHOENFELD
(214) 368-4007
8319 Preston Center Plaza
Dallas, TX 75225
Custom wedding bands

BURKE-LADDEN
GALLERY
(212) 786-9550
New York, NY

CAMILLA DIETZ
BERGERON LTD.
(212) 794-9100
New York, NY
Estate jewelry

CAROL SHUFRO
(212) 499-1921
New York, NY
**Wedding jewelry: rings, earrings,
necklaces**

THE CARROT TOP
at Lady Primrose's
(214) 871-8333
500 Crescent Court
Dallas, TX 75201
Antique jewelry

CATEN-MOORE
AT METROPOLITAN
DESIGN GROUP
(310) 458-3557
at Fred Segal Hoops,
Santa Monica, CA

CHRISTINE LIU
(713) 799-1199
Jewelry

THE CLAY POT
(800) 989-3579
162 7th Ave.
Brooklyn, NY 11215
Wedding bands, jewelry. Catalog

CLEAVAGE
(310) 657-2247
8522 Beverly Blvd., Room 673
Los Angeles, CA 90048

JEWELRY

COLLECTIVE
ANTIQUES
(415) 621-3800
212 Utah St.
San Francisco, CA 94103

CYNTHIA WOLFF
at Fragments
(212) 226-8878
New York, NY
Jewelry

DAVID CLAY JEWELERS
(415) 922-4339
1872 Union St.
San Francisco, CA 94123
Custom designs in platinum

DIANNE'S OLD AND
NEW ESTATES
(415) 346-7525
2181 Union St.
San Francisco, CA 94123
Antique jewelry

DUMONT
(310) 289-9500
8661 Sunset Blvd.
W. Hollywood, CA 90038
**Vintage jewelry, watches, gifts for
wedding party**

ELIZABETH RAND
(212) 754-1227
New York, NY
**Organic and contemporary
designs**

ERICKSON BEAMON
at Henri Bendel
(212) 247-1100
New York, NY
Earrings

GLORIA NATALE
(212) 769-4740
New York, NY
Custom wedding bands

HALTOM'S JEWELERS
(817) 336-4051
317 Main St.
Ft. Worth, TX 76102
Custom designs

JENNY LESSARD
(212) 966-7010
New York, NY
**Reproductions of ancient designs;
call for local availability**

KARA GAFFNEY
MCCANN
at Nieman-Marcus
(800) 944-9888
Jewelry

KEN RINEY ANTIQUES
& ESTATE JEWELRY
(214) 871-3640
500 Crescent Court, Ste. 154
Dallas, TX 75201
Antique jewelry

LANG
(415) 982-2213
323 Sutter St.
San Francisco, CA 94108
Antique and estate jewelry

LAURA MORTON
DESIGN
(310) 289-1166
Los Angeles, CA
Bridal collection; wedding sets

LISA MCKINZIE
JEWELRY
(925) 253-7505
P.O. Box 1905
Orinda, CA 94563

LOIS NULMAN STUDIO
(212) 794-8592
New York, NY
Jewelry

MANSOOR GORE
(650) 327-5667
530 Ramona St.
Palo Alto, CA 94325
Antique and custom jewelry

MARCIA LORBERFELD
(212) 354-7507
New York, NY
Gold and sterling silver bands

MARISSA
at La Lace
(310) 451-3557
1014 Montana Ave.
Santa Monica, CA 90403

THE MARLENE HARRIS
COLLECTION
(412) 828-1245
238 Freeport Road
Pittsburgh, PA 15238
Antique jewelry

MATTHEW
TRENT, INC.
(214) 871-9170
2530 Cedar Springs
Dallas, TX 75201
Custom and ready-made rings

MERYL WAITZ
(212) 675-7224
New York, NY
**Jewelry, gifts; call for local
availability**

MIGNON FAGET, LTD.
(504) 891-7545
710 Dublin St.
New Orleans, LA 70118
**Gold and sterling silver wedding
bands; call for local availability**

MIKIMOTO
(212) 586-7153
608 Fifth Ave.
New York, NY 10020
Pearls and jewelry

NANCY MARSHALL
at the Gazebo
(212) 832-7077
New York, NY

PARIS 1925
(415) 567-1925
1954 Union St.
San Francisco, CA 94123

PATIENCE MORGAN
JEWELRY
(914) 942-1894
Stony Point, NY
Custom designs

PROVERBS 31 (PEGGY
OLOUMI & CATHY
JOHNSTON)
(800) 655-4349
9114 Adams Ave., Suite 144
Huntington Beach, CA 92646
Heirlooms and reproductions

REINSTEIN/ROSS
(212) 226-4513
29 East 73rd. St.
New York, NY 10012
**Reproductions of ancient designs;
call for local availability**

SOMETHING OLD,
SOMETHING NEW
(201) 224-9224
Edgewater, NJ
**Wedding bands; specializing in
posy rings**

ST. ELIGIUS
(415) 771-2282
1748 Union St.
San Francisco, CA 94123

STEPHEN DWECK
(212) 764-3030
21 W. 38th St.
New York, NY 10018
Custom wedding bands

SUBTLE CREATURE
at Susan (415) 347-0452
San Francisco, CA

SUSAN CUMMINS
GALLERY
(415) 383-1512
12 Miller Ave.
Mill Valley, CA 94941

TAUBMAN, RUTH
(734) 995-4745
Wedding rings

TAIL OF THE YAK
(510) 841-9891
2632 Ashby Ave.
Berkeley, CA 94705
Custom jewelry

TIFFANY & CO.
(212) 755-8000
New York, NY
(310) 273-8880
Beverly Hills, CA
(415) 781-7000
San Francisco, CA
(214) 458-2800
Dallas, TX

TOUJOURS
(415) 346-3988
2484 Sacramento St.
San Francisco, CA 94115
Jewelry and bridal accessories

UNION STREET
GOLDSMITH
(415) 776-8048
1909 Union St.
San Francisco, CA 94108

WEDDING RING
ORIGINALS
(212) 751-3940
691 Lexington Ave.
New York, NY 10022

WELLS-WARE
(212) 222-9177
PO Box 1596
New York, NY 10023
**Custom jewelry and wedding
mementos**

GIFTS

ABC CARPET & HOME
(212) 473-3000
885 Broadway
New York, NY 10003
Housewares and gifts

ADC HERITAGE
(212) 750-2664
New York, NY

ANGÈLE PARLANGE
DESIGN
(504) 897-6511
5419 Magazine Street
New Orleans, LA 70115
**Table linens and accessories
for grooms and bridesmaids**

ANICHINI
(802) 889-9430
PO Box 67
Turnbridge, VT 05077
**Trousseau experts; call for local
availability**

ANN GISH
(805) 498-4447
Newbury Park, CA
**Silks and linens plus custom
work; call for local availability**

ANNIE GLASS
(408) 427-4260
109 Coopers St.
Santa Cruz, CA 95060
**Gifts, glassware and bridal
registry**

BACCARAT
(800) 363-4700
**Crystal and gifts; call for local
availability**

J. Mavic

BARBARA JERARD
JEWELRY DESIGN
(212) 628-4524
823 Park Ave.
New York, NY 10021
**Bridesmaids' gifts; heart
designs a speciality**

BERNARDAUD
(617) 696-2431
**China and giftware; call for local
availability**

BEVERLY CLARK
COLLECTION
(805) 566-1425
1120 Mark Avenue
Carpinteria, CA 93010
**Elegant bridal accessories.
Catalog**

BILTMORE ESTATE'S
GATEHOUSE GIFT
SHOP
Biltmore Estate
Asheville, NC
(828) 274-6220
**Elegant bridal accessories.
Catalog**

BOSE CORP.
(800) 444-2673
100 The Mountain
Framingham, MA 01701
Wave radios

Wells-Ware

BRAVURA
(415) 474-9092
2904 Octavia St.
San Francisco, CA 94123
Housewares

BRIAN WINDSOR ART, ANTIQUES, GARDEN FURNISHINGS
(212) 274-0411
272 Lafayette St.
New York, NY 10003

BROKEN CHINA JEWELRY
(830) 460-3373
HCR3 Box 955
Bandera, TX 78003

CALVIN KLEIN HOME COLLECTION
(800) 294-7978

CHINTZ & CO.
(407) 740-7224
515 N. Park Ave.
Winter Park, FL 32789
Vintage china, crystal, linens and sterling

CHURCHILL WEAVERS
at Gracious Home
(212) 988-8990
New York, NY

COLONIAL WILLIAMSBURG MAIL ORDER
(800) 446-9240
Williamsburg, VA
17th- and 18th-century style gifts. Catalog

DEBORAH SCHENCK
(802) 295-7916
13 Fox La.
Quechee, VT 05059
Framed artwork, decorative objects

DRANSFIELD & ROSS
(212) 741-7278
New York, NY
Linens; call for local availability

ELEMENTS/ JILL SCHWARTZ, INC.
(212) 243-2707
New York, NY
Custom jewelry; call for local availability

ERIKA READE LTD.
(404) 233-3857
3732 Roswell Rd., NE
Atlanta, GA 30342
Gifts

FIELDCREST CANNON
(800) 841-3336
Bed linens

FINO LINO
at Down & Quilt
(212) 423-9358
New York, NY
Linens

FISCHER TEXTILES
(619) 299-0772
205 16th St. Suite C
San Diego, CA 92101
Table linens; call for local availability

FOLLY
(212) 925-5012
13 White St.
New York, NY 10013
Antique garden accessories and benches

FORGET ME KNOTS
(415) 921-0838
1738 Union St.
San Francisco, CA 94123
Wedding favors

FRANCOISE NUNNALLE
(212) 246-4281
New York, NY
Vintage linens

GARDEN ANTIQUARY
(914) 737-6054
Cortland Manor, NY
Ornaments and fixtures in iron and stone; by appointment

THE GARDENER
(510) 548-4545
1836 Fourth St.
Berkeley, CA 94710
Ceramics, glass and garden accessories

GARDNER & BARR
(212) 752-0555
Venetian glass

GARNET HILL
(800) 622-6216
Natural fibers catalog

GODIVA CHOCOLATIER, INC.
(800) 9-Godiva
Call for local availability

HOLLYHOCK
(213) 931-3400
214 N. Larchmont Blvd.
Los Angeles, CA 90004
Interior design specializing in antiques

HOMESTEAD
(210) 997-5551
(800) 670-0729
223 East Main St.
Fredericksburg, TX 78624
Housewares

ILENE CHAZANOF
(212) 254-5564
New York, NY
Silver accessories

J. MAVEC & COMPANY, LTD
(212) 517-7665
946 Madison Ave.
New York, NY 10021
Small silver gifts

JUDI BOISSON AMERICAN COUNTRY
(516) 283-5466
134 Mariner Dr.
Southampton, NY11968
Folk furnishings. Catalog

JULIA GRAY LTD.
(212) 223-4454
Tables; call for local availability

KATE MORRISON
(412) 731-5196
5495 Bradlock Ave.
Pittsburgh, PA 15221
Made-to-order table linens, chair covers, aisle runners

KATHA DIDDEL HOME COLLECTION
(914) 381-0446
345 Fayette Ave.
Mamaroneck, NY 10543
Pillows

LA-DE-DA GIFTS
(609) 222-1778
129 Chester Ave.
Moorestown, NJ 08057
Home furnishings

LALIQUE
(800) 993-2580
René Lalique glassware

LA MAISON MODERNE
(212) 691-9603
144 W. 19 St.
New York, NY 10011
Home furnishings. Bridal registry available

LENOX
(609) 896-2800
China and giftware; call for local availability

LERON
(212) 249-3188
750 Madison Ave.
New York, NY 10021
Linens

THE LINEN GALLERY
(214) 522-6700
7001 Preston Rd.
Dallas, TX 75205

LLADRO
(800) 634-9088
Porcelain; call for local availability

MACKENZIE-CHILDS LTD.
(315) 364-7123
3260 State Rte. 90
Aurora, NY 13026
Tabletop, linens and home furnishings; call for local availability

MARINA MORRISON
(415) 781-7920
San Francisco, CA
Jewelry and bridesmaids' gifts

MEADOWSWEETS
(888) 827-6477
Middleburgh, NY
Crystalized flowers

MEG COHEN DESIGN
(212) 473-4002
New York, NY
Custom pillows, scarves; call for local availability

MON COEUR BY JANET BRUNO-SMALL
(504) 488-4775
422 S. Clark
New Orleans, LA 70119

MONTBLANC, INC.
(800) 995-4810
75 North St.
Bloomsbury, NJ 08804
Writing instruments

MOTTAHEDEH
(212) 685-3050
New York, NY
Majolica tableware; call for local availability

NAOMI'S ANTIQUES TO GO
(415) 775-1207
1817 Polk St.
San Francisco, CA 94109
American pottery, 1930-1960. Bridal registry available

NAY ET AL DESIGNS BY NAY
(310) 828-3166
Table linens

PALAIS ROYAL
(800) 207-5207
1725 Broadway St.
Charlottesville, VA 22902
Linens; call for local availability

PAPER WHITE LTD.
(415) 457-7673
P.O. Box 956
Fairfax, CA 94878
Linens and lace

PARIS
(212) 475-9755
New York, NY
Monograms; call for local availability

PARKER
(800) 237-8736
Writing instruments

PATRICK FREY/PARIS
at Rosaline Crowley
(203) 785-9376
Pillows

PEACOCK ALLEY
(214) 520-6736
3210 Armstrong
Dallas, TX 75205
Bed linens

PEKING HANDICRAFT
(800) 832-7727
Pillows

PETRUSHKA
(415) 626-7159
10 Brady St.
San Francisco, CA 94103

ROCOCO
(212) 673-7077
325 East 21st St.
New York, NY 10010
Jewelry, veils, pillows, gifts

ROOM SERVICE
(214) 369-7666
4354 Lovers Lane
Dallas, TX 75225
Vintage finds and furniture; design services

Rose Cottage

ROOM WITH A VIEW
(310) 453-7009
1600 Montana Ave.
Santa Monica, CA 90403
Linens

ROSE COTTAGE
(914) 737-1845
44 N. Division St.
Peekskill, NY 10566
**China, pillows, lampshades
and vintage throws**

ROSE TATTOO
(305) 293-1941
1114 White St.
Key West, FL 33040
**Gold-leafed containers, perfume
bottles; custom orders available**

ROYAL APPOINTMENTS
(847) 559-8111
2158 Northbrook Court
Northbrook, IL 60062
Victorian accessories

ROYAL DOULTON
(800) 682-4462
**China and giftware; call for local
availability**

RUE DE FRANCE
(800) 777-0998
Housewares and gifts

SHAXTED
(310) 273-4320
350 N. Camden Dr.
Beverly Hills, CA 90210
Linens

SPODE
(800) 631-7120
**China and giftware; call for local
availability**

THE STAMFORD
ANTIQUE CENTER
(888) 329-3546
735 Canal St.
Stamford, CT 06902

STONEWORKS
(800) STONE-61
Tuxedo, NJ
Custom engraved stones

STRATTON OF
LONDON
at Ye Old King's Head Shoppe
(310) 394-8765
132 Santa Monica Blvd.
Santa Monica, CA 90401
Gifts

SUE FISHER KING
(415) 922-7276
3067 Sacramento St.
and 375 Sutter St.
San Francisco, CA 94115
Linens and home furnishings

SUMMER HOUSE
(415) 383-6695
21 Throckmorton Ave.
Mill Valley, CA 94941

TRANSLATIONS
(214) 373-8391
4014 Villanova
Dallas, TX 75225
**Dinnerware, glassware and
flatware**

TREASURES FROM THE
PAST BY DOREEN
(212) 818-9078
211 W. 56th St.
New York, NY 10019
Antiques

TUDOR ROSE
ANTIQUES
(212) 677-5239
28 E. 10th St.
New York, NY 10003
Silver home accessories

ULLA DARNI, INC.
(518) 622-3566
Arca, NY
Hand-painted lamps

VANDERBILT AND CO.
(707) 963-1010
1429 Main St.
St. Helena, CA 94574
**French linens and home
furnishings**

VERTU
(214) 520-7817
4514 Travis Rd., Ste. 124
Dallas, TX 75205
**Fine china and flatware; bridal
registry**

WATERMAN
(800) 523-2486
Writing instruments

WATERFORD/
WEDGWOOD
(800) 677-7860
**China, crystal and giftware; call
for local availability**

WHITE LINEN
(914) 769-4551
520 Bedford Rd.
Pleasantville, NY 10570
Linens

WILLIAM YEOWARD
GLASS
(800) 818-8484
Gifts; call for local availability

PAPERS

ANNA GRIFFIN
DESIGN
(404) 817-8170
490 Armour Circle
Atlanta, GA 30324
Stationery

APIARY PRESS
(310) 450-3681
Santa Monica, CA
Albums and journals

ARAK KANOFSKY
STUDIOS
(201) 792-3458
111 First St.
Jersey City, NJ 07302
Custom invitations, favors

ARCH
(415) 433-2724
407 Jackson St.
San Francisco, CA 94133
Albums and journals

BETH RAMSEY
(402) 455-2514
6331 N. 32nd St.
Omaha, NE 68111
Bookbinding; by appointment

THE BEVERLEY
COLLECTION
(904) 387-2625
4217 Chippewa Drive
Jacksonville, FL 32210

BOHO DESIGNS
(415) 441-1617
San Francisco, CA
Custom invitations

BRETT LANDENBERGER
(415) 664-8015
2707 Judah St.
San Francisco, CA 94122
Albums and journals

CAMPBELL
STATIONERS &
ENGRAVERS
(214) 692-8380
8407 Pickwick Lane
Dallas, TX 75225

CARRIAGE HOUSE
PAPERS
(800) 669-8781
(718) 599-7857
79 Guernsey St.
Greenpoint, NY 10012
Handmade papers. Catalog

CLAUDIA LAUB
STUDIO
(213) 931-1710
7404 Beverly Blvd.
Los Angeles, CA 90036
Custom designs. Catalog

CRANE & CO.
(800) 472-7263
Stationery

CUSTOM CARD BAR
IN ELEMENTS
(714) 854-3690
4255 Campus Dr.
Irvine, CA 92612
Stationery and gifts

DECORATOR AND
CRAFT CORP.
(800) 835-3013
Papier-mâché boxes

DIEU DONNE
PAPERMILL
(212) 226-0573
433 Broome St.
New York, NY 10013
**Custom handmade papers, mono-
grams, and watermarks**

ELLEN SIMON
(317) 257-6968
5338 N. Pennsylvania St.
Indianapolis, IN 46220
**Invitations by hand or computer;
by appointment**

EMBREY PAPERS
(310) 440-2620
11965 San Vincente Blvd.
Los Angeles, CA 90049
Stationery

AN ENGLISHMAN IN
L.A.
(213) 656-8611
Los Angeles, CA
**Handmade and handlettered
invitations; illuminated wedding
certificates**

FITTERER, JACK
(518) 325-7172
1076 Collins St.
Hillsdale, NY 12529
Bookbinding

THE GARDENER
(510) 548-0838
1738 Union St.
San Francisco, CA 94123
Stationery

HENRY NUSS
BOOKBINDER INC.
(214) 747-5545
2701 Main St.
Dallas, TX 75226
Bookbinding

I.H.M. SYSTEMS
(516) 589-5600
518 Johnson Ave.
Bohemia, NY 11716
Engraving and embossing

THE ISLAND GALLERY
(770) 469-6683
951 B Main St.
Stone Mountain, GA 30083
Shadow boxes

J & M MARTINEZ
GRAPHIQUE DE
FRANCE
(800) 444-1464
9 State St. Woburn, MA 01801
**Letterpress; call for local
availability**

JUDY IVRY
(212) 677-1015
New York, NY
Embossed wedding albums

JUST ROBIN
(310) 273-9736
9171 Wilshire Blvd.
Beverly Hills, CA 90210
Stationery

KATE'S PAPERIE
(212) 941-9816
561 Broadway
New York, NY 10012
**Handmade papers and albums.
Custom invitations**

KEL-TOY
(510) 645-4885
San Francisco, CA
**Crafts and papers; call for local
availability**

KOZO
(415) 521-0869
531 Castro St.
San Francisco, CA 94114
Albums and journals

MADE BY MOTT
(212) 691-4170
New York, NY
Bookbinding

MARY NELL'S
(212) 865-8370
270 Riverside Dr. #9D
New York, NY 10025
**Wedding album and memorabilia
custom-designed**

NICOLE NASHBAN
(914) 626-5516
Westchester, NY
Bookbinding; by appointment

NINA OLSON
(212) 866-6634
733 Amsterdam Ave., #19J
New York, NY 10025
One-of-a-kind wedding collages

100TH MONKEY
PRODUCTIONS
(213) 745-4635
1933 South Broadway 356
Los Angeles, CA 90007
**Pre-printed stationery, Polaroid
transfer images**

PAPERS

PAPERS

OGGETTI
(415) 346-0631
1846 Union St.
San Francisco, CA 94123
Albums and journals

PAPER PLACE
(512) 451-6531
4001 N. Lamar
Austin, TX 78756

PAPER ROUTES
(214) 828-9494
404 Exposition
Dallas, TX 75226
Handmade papers

PAPYRUS
(800) 872-7978
Custom invitations, announcements, stationery and calligraphy

PAULA RUBENSTEIN
(440) 247-1906
37500 Jackson Rd.
Chagrin Falls, OH 44022
Stationery

PENDRAGON INC./
MARIA THOMAS
(508) 234-6843
27 Prospect St.
Whitinsville, MA 01588
Hand-lettered with hand-painted designs

PINE STREET PAPERY
(415) 332-0650
42-1/2 Caledonia St.
Sausalito, CA 94965

PRINTEMPS
(203) 226-6869
18 Avery Pl.
Westport, CT 06880
Custom stationers

THE PRINTERY
(516) 922-3250
43 W. Main St.
Oyster Bay, NY 11771
Custom invitations by hand and letterpress

PROMETHEUS
(714) 240-1052
Capistrano Beach, CA
Desk accessories, call for local availability

PROSE AND LETTERS
(408) 293-1852
San Jose, CA
Custom stationery and calligraphy; by appointment

PS THE LETTER
(817) 731-2032
5122 Camp Bowie Blvd.
Ft. Worth, TX 76107
Stationery

PURGATORY PIE PRESS
(212) 274-8228
19 Hudson St. #403
New York, NY 10013
Custom stationery made by hand letterpress; by appointment

RAY RIESER
(724) 335-5216
2900 Edgecliff Rd.
Lower Burrell, PA 15068
Stationery

THE RIBBONRY
(419) 872-0073
119 Louisiana Ave.
Perrysburg, OH 43551
Ribbons, accessories, books, and kits

RUFFLES
& FLOURISHES
(509) 627-5906
Richland, WI
Blind embossing, molded paper stationery; call for local availability

SCHURMAN FINE
PAPERS
(800) 333-6724
Stationery

SCRIPTURA
(504) 897-1555
5423 Magazine St.
New Orleans, LA 70115
Stationery

SILBERMAN-BROWN
STATIONERS
(206) 292-9404
1322 5th Ave.
Seattle, WA 98101
Invitations

SOHO REPRO
GRAPHICS
(212) 925-7575
69 Greene St.
New York, NY 10012
Custom stationery and graphic design

SOOLIP PAPERIE &
PRESS
(310) 360-0545
8646 Melrose Ave.
West Hollywood, CA 90069
Stationery

SOUTHERN
HEIRLOOMS BY EDIE
JORDAN
(601) 289-1815
305 N. Natchez, Suite G
Kosciusko, MS 39090
Albums and accessories

STEPHANNIE BARBA
(212) 426-8949
New York, NY
Wedding stationery with hand-painted flowers a speciality

STRAWBRIDGE
(415) 388-0235
86 Throckmorton Ave.
Mill Valley, CA 94941
Albums and journals

STRONG, MRS. JOHN L.
(212) 838-3848
699 Madison Ave.
New York, NY 10021
Engraving

T. ANTHONY
(212) 750-9797
(800) 722-2406
445 Park Ave.
New York, NY 10022
Specializing in leather albums. Catalog

TACTILE BOOKS
(212) 242-4320
New York, NY
Albums with specialty bindings

TALAS
(212) 219-0770
568 Broadway
New York, NY 10012
Bookbinding by appointment

TIFFANY & CO.
(415) 781-7000
350 Post St.
San Francisco, CA 94108
and (212) 755-8000
727 Fifth Ave.
New York, NY 10022

TRADE BINDERY
(415) 981-1856
355 Fremont
San Francisco, CA 94105
Bookbinding

TWO WOMEN
(415) 431-8805
San Francisco, CA
Gifts of paper; call for local availability

TWO WOMEN BOXING, INC.
(214) 939-1626
Dallas, TX
Silkscreen journals and gifts; call for local availability

WELDON DESIGN
(212) 925-4483
273 Church St.
New York, NY 10013
Engraving, printing, and calligraphy; by appointment only

WHERE YOUR HEART IS DESIGNS
(503) 359-4147
2313 A St.
Forest Grove, OR 97116
Hand-painted invitations, cards, programs, and home accessories

WILLIAM ERNEST BROWN STATIONERS
(214) 891-0008
Dallas, TX

WINSLOW PAPERS/ WYSTERIA PRESS
231 Lawrenceville Rd.
Lawrenceville, NJ 08648

WRITE SELECTION
(214) 750-0531
314 Preston Royal Center
Dallas, TX 75230

YESTERYEAR
(310) 278-2008
8816 Beverly Blvd.
Los Angeles, CA 90048
Shadow boxes

CALLIGRAPHY

ANNA PINTO
(201) 656-7402
Hoboken, NJ
Hand lettering and designs

BARBARA CALLOW CALLIGRAPHY
(415) 928-3303
1686 Union St.
San Francisco, CA 94123

CAROLE MAURER
(610) 642-9726
Wynnewood, PA
Typeface specialists

CHERYL JACOBSEN
(319) 351-6603
1131 E. Burlington St.
Iowa City, IA 52240
By appointment

CLAIRE MENDELSON
(212) 595-1775
New York, NY
(416) 784-1426
Toronto, Canada
Contemporary ketubah art and illustrations

ELEANOR WINTERS
(718) 855-7964
Brooklyn, NY
Lettering by hand and copper-plate; italics

HEIDI ADAMS
P.O. Box 444
Fredericksburg, TX 78624

JANET REDSTONE FINE CALLIGRAPHY & DESIGN
(312) 944-6624
(800) 484-7919 x3310
Chicago, IL
Monograms; brochure available

K2 DESIGN
(214) 522-2344
Dallas, TX

THE LETTERING DESIGN GROUP
(913) 362-7864
3520 W. 75 St., Suite 300
Prairie Village, KS 66208
Ornamental penmanship

MARGIE REED
(206) 232-7343
Seattle, WA

MEADOWSWEETS
(888) 827-6477
Middleburgh, NY
Floral and vine motifs

PAPINEAU CALLIGRAPHY
(510) 339-2301
5772 Thornhill Drive
Oakland, CA 94611
Calligraphy; by appointment

PENDRAGON, INC.
(508) 234-6843
Whitinsville, MA
Hand-lettered and hand-painted stationery

PROSE AND LETTERS
(408) 293-1852
351 Brookwood Dr.
San Jose, CA 95116

REGAL WRITINGS
(212) 252-4559
New York, NY
Invitations, announcements, menus and photo albums

RICHARD JORDAN
(212) 255-4511
New York, NY
Decorative painting and custom designs. Carolingian script

CEREMONY & CELEBRATION

ADAMS, MARJORIE PARROT
(978) 368-4225
P.O. Box 40
Lancaster, MA 01523
Decorative painter

M. BORGEN PAINTED GARDENS, INC.
(504) 641-8060
1732 Front St.
Slidell, LA 70458
Ceramicists

DARI GORDON AND BRUCE PIZZICHILLO
(510) 832.8380
2690 Union St.
Oakland, CA 94607
Specializing in handblown glass

DAVID LANDIS
(212) 563-7568
208 West 29th St., Room 613
New York, NY 10001-5206
**Crystal candlestick bobeches;
call for local availability**

ELIZABETH MEREDITH
(707) 763-1532
Petaluma, CA
**Decorative wedding accessories;
lighting a speciality. Call for local
availability**

ELIZABETH STREET
GALLERY
(212) 644-6969
1176 Second Ave.
New York, NY 10021
**Specializing in antique
architectural remnants
and garden fixtures**

THE GARDENER
(510) 548-4545
1836 Fourth St.
Berkeley, CA 94710
Garden accessories

GARY HALSEY
(718) 398-7521
Brooklyn, NY
Decorative painter

IAN AND JO LYDIA
CRAVEN POTTERY
(800) 764-2402
1692 Highway 80 South
Micaville, NC 28755

MARY ROSE YOUNG
(011) 44-1225-44899
6 London St.
Bath BA1 5BU
England

MOMBASA CANOPIES
(800) 641-2345
2345 Fort Worth St.
Grand Prairie, TX 75050
Canopies

SALT MARSH POTTERY
(800) 859-5028
1167 Russells Mill Rd.
South Dartmouth, MA 02748

THOMAS PRETI
CATERING
(718) 764-3188
38-03 24th St.
Long Island City, NY 11101

VANDERBILT AND CO.
(707) 963-1010
1429 Main St.
St. Helena, CA 94574
Home accessories and pottery

WEEPING CHERUB
(800) 352-5915
PO Box 207
Essex, NY 12936

WHICHFORD POTTERY
(011) 44-1608-684-416
Whichford, Shipston-on-Stour
Warwickshire CV36 5PG
England

PHOTOGRAPHY

ANTHONY ISRAEL
(718) 832-1976
566 9th St.
Brooklyn, NY 11215

BABBONI'S CREATIVE
IMAGING
(414) 328-3211
8306 W. Lincoln Ave.
West Allis, WI 53219

BACHARACH
PHOTOGRAPHS
(617) 536-4730
647 Boylston St.
Boston, MA 02116

BERLINER STUDIOS
(213) 857-1282
314 N. LaBrea Ave.
Los Angeles, CA 90036

BISSELL
PHOTOGRAPHY
(440) 247-7988
Cleveland, OH

BRESNER STUDIOS
(215) 546-7277 6729 Castor Ave.
Philadelphia, PA 19149
and 210 West Rittenhouse Square,
Suite 401
Philadelphia, PA 19103

CHRIS HARTLOVE
(410) 426-2829
Washington, D.C.

CHRISTINE RODIN
(212) 242-3260
New York, NY

CILENTO BY
LIFETOUCH
(414) 964-6161
1400 E. Capital Dr.
Milwaukee, WI 53217

DENIS REGGIE
(404) 873-8080
75 14th St. NE, Ste. 2120
Atlanta, GA 30309

EVAN KAFKA
(718) 349-6987
106 Jackson St.
Brooklyn, NY 11211

FRED MARCUS
(212) 873-5588
245 W. 72nd St.
New York, NY 10023

GREVY PHOTOGRAPHY
(504) 522-9825
7433 Maple St.
New Orleans, LA 70118

HAL SILFER
(800) 234-7755
(617) 787-7910
Boston, MA

HEIRLOOM
RESTORATION
(203) 795-0565
218 Hemlock Hill Rd.
Orange, CT 06477

HILARY N. BULLOCK
(612) 338-7516
529 S. 7th St., Ste. 555
Minneapolis, MN 55415

HOLGER THOSS
(212) 627-8829
180 Varick St., Studio 400
New York, NY 10014

JACK CAPUTO
PHOTOGRAPHY AND
VIDEO PRODUCTIONS
(310) 273-6181
4735 Sepulveda Blvd. #422
Sherman Oaks, CA 91403

JAMES FRENCH
(214) 368-0990
8411 Preston Ave., Suite 555
Dallas, TX 75225

JAMIE BOSWORTH
(503) 246-5378
8635 SW 9th St.
Portland, OR 97219

JEANNIE FREY RHODES
(504) 343-8080
2375 Myrtle Ave.
Baton Rouge, LA 70806

JOHN DERRYBERRY
AND ASSOCIATES
(214) 357-5457
5757 W. Lovers Ln., Suite 310
Dallas, TX 75209

JOHN TILLEY
(214) 358-4747
4551 W. Lovers Ln.
Dallas, TX 75209

JOHN WOLFSOHN
(310) 859-9266
9904 Durant Dr.
Beverly Hills, CA 90212

JULIE SKARRATT
(212) 877-2604
160 W. 73rd St., #11B
New York, NY 10023

KAISH DAHL
(310) 724-7282
9400 Santa Monica Blvd.
Beverly Hills, CA 90210

KEITH TRUMBO
(212) 580-7104
New York, NY

LEAH CAMPBELL
(612) 872-1102
2445 Lyndale Ave.
Minneapolis, MN 55403

LONGSHOTS
PHOTOGRAPHY
(504) 282-3559
1505 Gardena Dr.
New Orleans, LA 70122

MALLORY SAMSON
(212) 673-0668
New York, NY
(415) 332-3696
Sausalito,CA

MARGARET BRAUN
(212) 929-1582
New York, NY

MAUREEN EDWARDS
DEFRIES
(203) 740-9343
Brookfield, CT

NELSON HUME
(212) 222-7424
New York, NY

PHIL KRAMER
(215) 928-9189
30 S. Bank St.
Philadelphia, PA 19106

ROB FASER
(212) 941-0433
13-17 Laight St.
New York, NY 10013

ROBERT FRIEDEL
(212) 477-3542
New York, NY

ROBERT GEORGE
(314) 771-6622
1933 Edwards Ave.
St. Louis, MO 63110

ROBIN SACHS
(214) 824-0624
Dallas, TX

ROMAN IWASIWKA
(914) 626-3845
Kerhonkson, NY

ROSS WHITAKER/
TERRY ROY GRUBER
(212) 262-9777
315 W. 57th St., #18C
New York, NY 10019

SENGBUSH
PHOTOGRAPHY
(214) 363-3264
6611 Snyder Plaza, Ste. 109
Dallas, TX 75205

STEVEN E. GROSS AND
ASSOCIATES
(312) 243-1979
555 W. 18th St.
Chicago, IL 60616

SUSAN BLOCH
(516) 549-0203
59 Goen Na Little Trail
Huntington, NY 11743

VALERIE SHAFF
(212) 475-2819
New York, NY

WENDI SCHNEIDER
(303) 322-2246
1635 Hudson St.
Denver, CO 80220

ZALEWA DESIGNER
IMAGES
(800) 836-7688
(812) 951-3259
9700 State Rd. 64
Georgetown, IN 47122

WEDDING CAKES

ANA PAZ CAKES
(305) 471-5850
1460 NW 107th Ave., Unit D
Miami, FL 33172

ANN AMERNICK
(301) 718-0434
Chevy Chase, MD

ASHLEY BAKERY
(803) 763-4125
Charleston, SC

AUGUST THOMSEN
CORPORATION
(800) 645-7170
(516) 676-7100
36 Seacliff Ave.
Glencove, NY 11542
Cake-making supplies. Catalog

Gail Watson Custom Cakes

BETH HIRSCH
(212) 941-8085
New York, NY

BETTINA THOMPSON
STERN
(202) 244-5903
Washington, D.C.

CHERYL KLEINMAN
CAKES
(718) 237-2271
448 Atlantic Ave.
Brooklyn, NY 11215

CLASSIC CAKES
(317) 844-6901
Indianapolis, IN

COLUMBUS BAKERY
(212) 421-0334
9057 First Ave.
New York, NY 10022

CRAVINGS
(314) 961-3534
8149 Big Bend
Welster Groves, MO 63119

CREATIVE CAKES
(803) 744-6791
Charleston, SC

CUPCAKE CAFE
(212) 465-1530
522 Ninth Ave.
New York, NY 10018

DIANE'S BAKERY
(516) 621-2522
23 Bryant Ave.
Roslyn, NY 11576

DONALD WRESSEL
(310) 273-2222
Los Angeles, CA

GAIL PEACHIN
(607) 397-9700
HCR 33
Charlottesville, NY 12036

GAIL WATSON
CUSTOM CAKES
(212) 967-9167
335 W. 38th St.
New York, NY 10018

HANSEN CAKES
(213) 936-4332
1072 S. Fairfax Ave.
Los Angeles, CA 90019

ISN'T THAT SPECIAL
OUTRAGEOUS CAKES
(201) 216-0123
720 Monroe St.
Hoboken, NJ 07030

JANE STACEY
(505) 473-1243
Santa Fe, NM

JESSICA BARTL
(612) 829-0673
Minneapolis, MN

LA CUISINE, THE
COOK'S RESOURCE
(800) 521-1176
323 Cameron St.
Alexandria, VA 22314
Baking supplies. Catalog

LA FLUTE GANA
(011) 331-435-84262
226 Rue Des Pyrenees
75020 Paris France

LE GATEAU CAKERY
(214) 528-6102
3128 Harvard
Dallas, TX 75205

LE ROYALE ICING BY
MARGARET LASTICK
(708) 386-4175
35 Chicago Ave.
Oak Park, IL 60302

LES FRIANDISES
(212) 988-1616
972 Lexington Ave.
New York, NY 10021

MICHEL RICHARD
(310) 275-5707
310 S. Robertson Blvd.
Los Angeles, CA 90048

THE NUTCRACKER
SWEET SHOP
(412) 963-7951
1215 North Canal St.
Pittsburgh, PA 15215

PATISSERIE LANCIANI
(212) 989-1213
414 West 14th St.
New York, NY 10014

PATTICAKES
(818) 794-1128
1900 N. Allen Ave.
Altadena, CA 91001
By appointment

A PIECE OF CAKE
(803) 881-2034
Charleston, SC

THE PINK ROSE
PASTRY SHOP
(215) 592-9321
630 S. Fourth St.
Philadelphia, PA 19147

POLLY'S CAKES
(503) 230-1986
25 NW 23rd Place, Suite #269
Portland, OR 97210
By appointment

RON BEN-ISRAEL
(212) 627-2418
New York, NY

ROSEMARY'S CAKES,
INC.
(201) 833-2417
299 Rutland Ave.
Teaneck, NJ 07666

ROSIE'S CREATIONS,
INC.
(212) 362-6069
New York, NY
Cake toppers

SIMA'S
(414) 257-0998
817 N. 60th St.
Milwaukee, WI 53213

A SPIRITED CAKE
(214) 522-2212
14819 Inwood Rd.
Dallas, TX 75044

SUD FINE PASTRY
(215) 592-0499
801 E. Passyunk Ave.
Philadelphia, PA 19147

SUGAR BOUQUETS
(800) 203-0629
(973) 538-3542
23 North Star Drive
Morristown, NJ 07960
**Cake making lessons and
supplies. Catalog**

SUSAN KENNEDY
CHOPSON
(615) 865-2437
Madison, TN

SWEET DREAMS
(901) 725-1265
1441 Jackson St.
Memphis, TN 38107

SWEET SISTERS
(201) 478-2650
157 5th St.
Clifton, NJ 07011

SYLVIA WEINSTOCK
CAKES
(212) 925-6698
273 Church St.
New York, NY 10013
By appointment

A TASTE OF EUROPE
BY GISELA
(817) 654-9494
4817 Brentwood Stair
Fort Worth, TX 76103

VANILLA BEAN BAKERY
(847) 446-5444
301 South Happ Rd.
Northfield, IL 60093

WEDDING CAKES
BY MERIBETH
(919) 846-5454
Raleigh, NC

FLOWERS

ALEXANDRA RANDALL
FLOWERS
(516) 862-9291
St. James, NY
**Herbs, garden flowers a specialty;
by appointment**

ANDREW PASCOE
FLOWERS
(516) 922-9561
Oyster Bay, NY
By appointment; will travel

ANTHONY GARDEN
BOUTIQUE LTD.
(212) 737-3303
134 E. 70th St.
New York, NY 10021
Wedding planning

ARRANGEMENT
(305) 576-9922
3841 NE 2nd Ave., Suite 403
Miami, FL 33137
Custom design

ATELIER, A WORK
SHOP
(214) 750-7622
3419 Milton Ave.
Dallas, TX 75205
Custom design

ATLANTA FLOWER
MARKET
(770) 396-3301
6427 Roswell Rd.
Atlanta, GA 30328

BAUMGARTEN
KRUEGER
(414) 276-2382
225 E. Wisconsin Ave.
Milwaukee, WI 53202

BLONG FLORISTS
(904) 389-7661
4207 St. Johns Ave.
Jacksonville, FL 32210

BLOOMERS
(415) 563-3266
2975 Washington St.
San Francisco, CA 94115

BLOSSOMS
(248) 644-4411
175 W Maple Rd.
Birmingham, MI 48072

BOMARZO
(415) 771-9111
1410 Vallejo St.
San Francisco, CA 94109
**Hand-wired bouquets; by
appointment**

BOTANICA
(901) 274-5767
937 S. Cooper St.
Memphis, TN 38103
**Architectural and naturalistic
garden styles**

BOTANICALS
ON THE PARK
(800) 848-7674
(314) 772-7674
3014 South Grand
St. Louis, MO 63118

BOUQUETS
(303) 333-5500
1525 Fifteenth St.
Denver, CO 80202

BRADY'S FLORAL
DESIGN
(602) 945-8776
(800) 782-6508
4167 N. Marshall Way
Scottsdale, AZ 85251

BRUNET, CAROLE
(973) 746-4465
Montclair, NJ
**Foliage, organic materials; by
appointment**

CALABRIA
(212) 675-2688
New York, NY

CAROLYN BLAZIER
(770) 893-3767
Alpharetta, GA
Vintage silk flowers

CASTLE & PIERPONT
(212) 570-1284
401 E. 76th St.
New York, NY 10021

CENTRAL FLORIST
(212) 686-7952
40 W. 28th St.
New York, NY 10001
Tools and supplies

CHARLES RADCLIFF
(713) 522-9100
1759 Richmond Ave.
Houston, TX 77098

CHARLESTON FLORIST
(803) 577-5691
184 King St.
Charleston, SC 29407

Christian Tortu

CHRISTIAN TORTU
at Takashimaya
(212) 350-0100
693 Fifth Ave.
New York, NY 10022
**Unusual combinations,
containers**

CHRISTOPHER
BASSETT
(212) 254-0685
New York, NY
**Organic materials, handwired
bouquets**

CINDERELLA
(212) 840-0644
60 W. 38th St.
New York, NY 10018
**Silk flowers, ribbons, trimmings.
Catalog**

COCO & CO., INC.
(214) 748-1899
2100 Stemmans Freeway
Dallas, TX 75207

COLUMBINE
(415) 434-3016
1541 Grant St.
San Francisco, CA 94133

THE COTTAGE
GARDEN
(404) 233-2050
2973 Hardman Ct.
Atlanta, GA 30305.

COUNTRY GARDENS
(440) 333-3763
Cleveland, OH

COVENT GARDENS
(513) 232-4422
6209 Corbley
Mt. Washington, OH 45230

CRAIG SOLE DESIGNS
(913) 649-9299
7928 Conser St.
Overland Park, KS 66204

THE CREST OF FINE
FLOWERS
(847) 256-3900
417 Fourth St.
Wilmette, IL 60091
By appointment

CYNTHIA'S CREATIONS
(303) 699-5938
2727 S. Lewiston St.
Aurora, CO 80013

CYNTHIA'S FLORAL
DESIGNS
(800) 944-8246
3915 Hendricks Ave.
Jacksonville, FL 32207

D'CLEMENTS
(303) 399-5543
909 S. Oneida St.
Denver, CO 80224
By appointment

DAVID BROWN
FLORIST
(713) 521-1191
4622 Centre St.
Houston, TX 77006

DELAPGAR
(513) 321-2600
3433 Michigan Ave.
Cincinnati, OH 45208

DESIGNS BY JODY
(847) 816-6661
152 Baker Rd.
Lake Bluff, IL 60044
By appointment

DEVONSHIRE
(561) 833-0796
340 4th Ave.
Palm Beach, FL 33480

DIANE JAMES SILK
FLOWER DESIGNS
(203) 655-4195
11 Shennamere Rd.
Darien, CT 06820

DONALD
VANDERBROOK
(216) 371-0164
1898 South Taylor Rd.
Cleveland Heights, OH 44118.

DOROTHY BIDDLE
SERVICE
(717) 226-3239
U.S. Rt. 6
Greeley, PA 18425
Catalog

DULKEN & DERRICK
(212) 929-3614
12 W. 21st St.
New York, NY 10011
Herbs, baskets, handmade flowers

ELLEN MCCLELLAND
LESSER
P.O. Box 151
Stuyvesant, NY 12173
Silk flowers

ELIZABETH HOUSE
(704) 342-3919
1431 S. Blvd.
Charlotte, NC 28203

EMILIA'S FLOWERS
(801) 943-7301
702 East & 123 South
Draper, UT 84020

ENGLISH GARDEN
(615) 269-0197
Nashville, TN
By appointment

ESPRIT DE FLEUR
(206) 547-7271
Seattle, WA
By appointment only

EVERYDAY GARDENER
(601) 981-0273
2945 Old Canton Rd.
Jackson, MS 39216
Garden accessories

FIORI
(612) 623-1153
17 NE 5th St.
Minneapolis, MN 55413

FLORAL DECOR BY
KEN & LISA GIBBONS
(201) 217-0924
Jersey City, NJ
**Fresh and dried bouquets,
topiaries, decorative items**

FLORALS OF
WATERFORD
(201) 327-0337
74 E. Allendale Rd.
Saddle River, NJ 07458
**Flowers, fruits, unusual
combinations, antique accessories**

FLORAMOR STUDIO
FLORIST
(415) 864-0145
569 Seventh St.
San Francisco, CA 94103
By appointment

FLORA NOVA
(503) 228-1134
1302 NW Hoyt
Portland, OR 97209

FLORIDELLA
(415) 775-4065
1920 Polk St.
San Francisco, CA 94109

FLORIST GRAND
(808) 599-4132
705 S. King St., Suite 100
Honolulu, HI 96813

THE FLOWER STUDIO
(414) 228-9200
6933 N. Port Washington Rd.
Milwaukee, WI 53217

FLOWERS ON THE
SQUARE
(817) 429-2888
311 Main St.
Fort Worth, TX 76102

FOLIAGE GARDEN
(212) 989-3089
120 W. 28th St.
New York, NY 10001
**Flowering plants and trees;
to buy or rent**

FRED PALMER
FLOWERS
(505) 820-0044
2214 W. Alameda, Box F
Santa Fe, NM 87501

FRIENDLY FLOWER
GALLERY
(919) 596-8747
2208 Halloway
Durham, NC 27703

GALVESTON WREATH
COMPANY
(409) 765-8597
1124 25th Galveston, TX
Dried botanicals, berries, flowers

GARDEN STORE
(801) 595-6622
678 South 700 East
Salt Lake City, UT 84102

THE GARDENER
(510) 548-4545
1836 Fourth St.
Berkeley, CA 94710
Garden accessories

GARDENER'S EDEN
(800) 822-9600
San Francisco, CA
**Catalog for garden supplies,
containers, greenery**

GARY PAGE
WHOLESALE FLOWERS
(212) 741-8928
New York, NY
**Local and imported flowers,
foliage**

THE GIFT HUT
(216) 777-3688
22086 Lorain Rd.
Fairview Park, OH 44126

GLORIMUNDI
(212) 727-7090
307 Seventh Ave.
New York, NY 10001
Floral, event design

GRASSROOTS GARDEN
(212) 226-2662
131 Spring St.
New York, NY 10012
Plants, trees, supplies

HASTINGS &
HASTINGS
(415) 381-1272
27 Miller Ave.
Mill Valley, CA 94941

HEPATICA
(412) 241-3900
1119 S. Braddock Ave.
Pittsburgh, PA 15218

HIBISCUS
(816) 891-0808
10010 N. Executive Hills Blvd.
Kansas City, MO 64153

HOLLIDAY'S
FLOWERS, INC.
(901) 753-2400
2316 S. Germantown Rd.
Germantown, TN 38138

StoneKelly

INCLINE FLORIST
(800) 556-5033
(702) 831-5043
850 Tanager St.
Incline Village, NV 89450

INDIGO V.
(415) 647-2116
1352 Castro
San Francisco, CA 94114
By appointment

IN SITU FLOWERS
(212) 861-5316
219 E. 81 St.
New York, NY 10021

JACOB MAARSE
(626) 449-0246
655 E. Green St.
Pasadena, CA 91101

JANE PRUITT
(912) 925-9849
Savannah, GA

JENNIFER HOUSER
(516) 725-2667
Sag Harbor, NY

JOSEPH MAAKE
FLOWERS &
DECORATIVE
ACCESSORIES
(516) 921-3076
Oyster Bay, NY
Fresh and dried flowers

JUDITH BRANDLEY
FLORIST OF SIERRA
MADRE
(626) 355-6972
Sierra Madre, CA
By appointment

KINSMAN COMPANY
(800) 733-4146
PO Box 357, River Road Point
Pleasant, PA 18950
**Complete line of garden
accessories. Catalog**

KIYBELE CREATIONS
(914) 273-6659
Armonk, NY
**Garden accessories; call for local
availability**

L. BECKER FLOWERS
(212) 439-6001
217 E. 83rd St.
New York, NY 10028
Bridal bouquets

LARKSPUR
(612) 332-2140
514 N. Third St.
Minneapolis, MN 55401

LAURELS CUSTOM
FLORIST
(213) 655-3466
7964 Melrose Ave.
Los Angeles, CA 90046
Event planning; by appointment

LAURIE STERN
FLORAL ART
(510) 528-8040
El Cerrito, CA 94530
**Victorian and English country
style flowers and greeting cards;
by appointment**

LESLIE PALME
(718) 622-6995
Brooklyn, NY
By appointment

LIVING CREATIONS
(801) 485-3219
Snowbird, UT

MAGNOLIAS
(502) 585-4602
Louisville, KY

MAIN STREET
FLORAGARDENS
(415) 485-2996
P.O. Box 686
San Anselmo, CA 94979
By appointment

THE MARKETPLACE
(212) 594-8289
245 W. 29th St.
New York, NY 10012
Rentals

MARK HALL OF THE
RENAISSANCE GARDEN
(617) 536 6937
Boston, MA

MARSH MEADOWS
DESIGN
(912) 925-9849
13214 Whitebluff Rd.
Savannah, GA 31419

MARSHA D. HECKMAN
(415) 388-2295
Mill Valley, CA

METALCRAFTS
(703) 335-6060
802 Centerville Rd.
Manassas, VA 22111
**Copper containers, metal pails,
vases**

MICHAEL HALEY LTD.
(904) 387-3000
3953 St. Johns Ave.
Jacksonville, FL 32205

MIHO KOSUDA LTD.
(212) 922-9122
310 E. 44th St.
New York, NY 10017
Hand-wired bouquets

MITCH'S FLOWERS
(504) 899-4843
4843 Magazine St.
New Orleans, LA 70115

MOSKATEL'S
(213) 689-4830
738 S. Wall St.
Los Angeles, CA 90014
Crafts

MUNDER-SKILES
(212) 717-0150
799 Madison Ave., 3rd Fl.
New York, NY 10021
**Reproduction garden ornaments,
furniture; custom work**

NANZ AND KRAFT
FLORIST
(502) 897-6551
141 Breckinridge Ln.
Louisville, KY 40207

NATURE'S DAUGHTER
(908) 221-0258
Basking Ridge, NJ
Event planning; by appointment

NEW ENGLAND
GARDEN ORNAMENTS
(508) 867-4474
North Brookfield, MA
Garden structures; catalog

NICOLE ESPOSITO
FLORAL DESIGNS
(212) 787-0067
321 W. 80th St. #7
New York, NY 10024,
By appointment

PALMER-KELLY
FLORAL DESIGNS
(317) 923-9903
5168 N. College Ave.
Indianapolis, IN 46205

PARNY SILK FLOWERS
(212) 645-9526
146 W. 28th St.
New York, NY 10001
Silk and paper flowers

PETER A. CHOPIN
FLORIST, INC.
(504) 891-4455
2800 St. Charles Ave.
New Orleans, LA 70115

POTTED GARDENS
(212) 255-4797
27 Bedford St.
New York, NY 10013
and (516) 537-6235
Route 27 (Montauk Highway)
and Poxabogue
Bridgehampton, NY
Unusual containers

PRESTON BAILEY
(212) 683-0035
New York, NY

QUENTIN NATURAL
MATERIALS
(409) 258-5744
Dayton, TX
Dried local berries, grasses

R. H.
(415) 346-1460
2506 Sacramento St.
San Francisco, CA 94115
Garden and home accessories

RAYON VERT
EXTRAORDINARY
FLOWERS
(415) 861-3516
3187 16th St.
San Francisco, CA 94103
Decorative accessories

REGALO FLOWERS
(505) 983-4900
150 Washington Ave.
Santa Fe, NM 87501

REIKO M.
(810) 543-5433
619 S. Washington
Royal Oak, MI 48067

ROBERT BOZZINI
(415) 351-2823
San Francisco, CA

ROLLING HILLS
FLOWER MART
(310) 540-3333
1763 South Elena
Redondo Beach, CA 90277

ROSEDALE NURSERY
(914) 769-1300
51 Saw Mill River Rd.
Hawthorne, NY 10532
**Garden supplies, landscaping
services**

ROSEWOOD FLORISTS
(803) 256-8351
2917 Rosewood Dr.
Columbia, SC 29205

SALUTATIONS INK
(303) 371-2393
5005 Peoria St.
Denver, CO 80239

SILVER BIRCHES
CUSTOM DESIGN
FLORISTRY
(626) 796-1431
477 South Raymond Ave.
Pasadena, CA 91005

STACEY DANIELS
FLOWERS
(800) 463-7632
42 Ganung Dr.
Ossining, NY 10562
**English garden style, by
appointment**

STANLEY'S GARDEN
WORKS
(415) 567-6476
San Francisco, CA

STONEKELLY
(212) 875-0500
328 Columbus Ave.
New York, NY 10023

SUZANNE CODI
(202) 269-4259
111 Quincy Place NE
Washington, DC 20002

THRAN'S FLOWERS
(702) 588-1661
225 Kingsley Grade
Stateline, NV 89449

TIM CONDRON
(412) 361-4057
5879 Center Ave.
Pittsburgh, PA 15206

TOMMY LUKE FLORIST
(503) 228-3131
1701 SW Jefferson St.
Portland, OR 97205

TOMMY THOMPSON
(313) 665-4222
504 South Main St.
Ann Arbor, MI 48103

TREILLAGE
(212) 535-2288
418 E. 75th St.
New York, NY 10021
**Garden ornaments, weathered
furniture, accessories**

TROCHTA'S FLOWERS
AND GREENHOUSES
(800) 232-7307
(405) 848-3338
6700 N. Broadway
Oklahoma City, OK 73116

THE TULIP TREE
(615) 352-1466
6025 Highway 100
Nashville, TN 37205
Flowers and gifts

TWO DESIGN GROUP
(214) 741-3145
Dallas, TX
Planning

TZIN TZUN TZAN
(415) 641-0373
1570 Indiana St.
San Francisco, CA 94107
Decorative folk accessories

UPTOWN FLOWERS
(504) 899-2923
538 Nashville Ave.
New Orleans, LA 70115

URBAN ARCHAEOLOGY
(212) 431-6969
285 Lafayette St.
New York, NY 10012
**Garden, architectural objects;
for purchase or rent**

VALORIE HART
DESIGNS
(408) 720-9506
Sunnyvale, CA
Full-service planning

VANDERBILT AND CO.
(707) 963-1010
1429 Main St.
St. Helena, CA 94574
Baskets for inside and out

VINES
(505) 820-7770
459 Cerrillos Rd.
Sante Fe, NM 87501

VERY SPECIAL
FLOWERS
(212) 206-7236
New York, NY
**Full-service planning,
sculptural designs**

WATERFORD GARDENS
(201) 327-0337
Saddle River, NJ
Water lilies

WELLS FLOWERS
(317) 872-4267
2160 W. 86th St.
Indianapolis, IN 46260

WHOLESALE DRIED
FLOWERS
(415) 781-3034
149 Morris St.
San Francisco, CA 94107

WILDFLOWERS OF
LOUISVILLE
(502) 584-3412
500 S. Fourth Ave.
Louisville, KY 40202

WINSTON FLORIST
(617) 541-1100
160 Southampton St.
P.O. Box 933
Boston, MA 02117

WISTERIA DESIGN
(612) 332-0633
275 Market St., Suite 50
Minneapolis, MN 55405

ZÉZÉ FLOWERS
(212) 753-7767
395 East 52nd St.
New York, NY 10022

SITES

ADAMSON HOUSE
(310) 457-8185
23200 Pacific Coast Hwy.
Malibu, CA 90265
Groomed garden

THE ADOLPHUS
HOTEL
(214) 742-8200
1321 Commerce St.
Dallas, TX 75202

ALDEN YACHT
CHARTER
(800) 253-3654
(401) 683-1782
Portsmouth, RI 02871
Yachts to charter

ALLEN HOUSE
(248) 642-2817
556 W. Maple Rd.
Birmingham, MI 48001
18th-century house with gardens

THE AMERICA
SOCIETY
(212) 249-8950
680 Park Ave.
New York, NY 10021
**Latin-American landmark
residence**

ARBORETUM OF LOS
ANGELES COUNTY
(818) 821-3286
301 N. Baldwin Ave.
Arcadia, CA 91006

ARCHBISHOP'S
MANSION
(415) 563-7872
1000 Fulton St.
San Francisco, CA

ARIZONA BILTMORE
(602) 954-2540
24th & Missouri Ave.
Phoenix, AZ 85016

ATLANTA BOTANICAL
GARDENS
(404) 876-5859 ext. 224
P.O. Box 77246
Atlanta, GA 30357

BECK CHAPEL
(812) 855-7425
University Chancellor's Office
Owen Hall, Rm. 100
Indiana University
Bloomington, IN 47405
Campus chapel

BANNING RESIDENCE
MUSEUM
(310)548-7777
401 E. M. St.
Wilmington, CA 90748
1864 mansion

THE BILTMORE
ESTATE
(800) 408-4405
1 North Pack Square
Asheville, NC 28801
**Historic 250-room mansion on
8000-acre estate**

THE BILTMORE HOTEL
(305) 445-1926
1200 Anastasia Ave.
Coral Gables, FL 33134
**1926 Mediterranean/Spanish
style hotel with ballroom**

BISHOP'S LODGE
(505) 983-6377
Bishop's Lodge Rd.
Sante Fe, NM 87504
Mountain chapel and inn

THE BLANTYRE
(413) 637-3556
16 Blantyre Rd., P.O.Box 995
Lenox, MA 01240
**Restored 1900's era Scottish
Tudor mansion on 100-acre
estate**

BOETTCHER MANSION
(303) 526-0855
900 Colorow Rd.
Golden, CO 80401
**1917 Arts and Crafts
mansion/hunting lodge on 110
forested acres**

BOTSFORD BRIAR
(914) 831-6099
19 High St.
Beacon, NY 12508
**Victorian mansion with riverview
balcony, for small gatherings**

THE BOUCVALT
HOUSE
(504) 528-9771
1025 St. Louis St.
New Orleans, LA 70118
Historic French Quarter home

BOULDERS INN
(860) 868-0541
Route 45
New Preston, CT
Small lakefront weddings

CAFFE ROSSO
(212) 633-9277
284 W. 12th St.
New York, NY 10014

CAMBERLY BROWN
HOTEL
(502) 583-1234
335 W. Broadway St.
Louisville, KY 40202

THE CAPTAIN
WHIDBEY INN
(360) 678-4097
2072 W. Captain Whidbey Inn Rd.
Coupeville, WA 98239
Coastline inn

CARNEGIE MUSEUMS
OF PITTSBURGH
(412) 622-3360
4400 Forbes Ave.
Pittsburgh, PA 15213
Marble-columned music hall

CASTLE HILL
(978) 356-4351
290 Argilla Rd.
Ipswich, MA 01938
1910 hilltop estate

CENTRAL PARK
CONSERVANCY
(212) 360-2766
5th and 105th St.
New York, NY
Formal gardens, terraces

CENTURY INN
(412) 945-6600
National Road
Scenery Hill, PA 15360

CHALKERS
(415) 512-0450
101 Spear St.
1 Rincon Center
San Francisco, CA 94105

CHARLES ORVIS INN
AT THE EQUINOX
(802) 362-4700
Historic Rte. 7A
Manchester Village, VT 05254

CHARLES TOWN
LANDING
(803) 852-4200
1500 Old Towne Rd.
Charleston, SC 29407
Late 1800's plantation garden

CHARMING INNS INC.
(843) 722-8680
212 1/2 King St.
Charleston SC 29401
Ballrooms and formal gardens

CHEEKWOOD
BOTANICAL GARDENS
(615) 353-2148
1200 Forrest Park Drive
Nashville, TN 37205

CINCINNATIAN HOTEL
(513) 381-3000
601 Vine St.
Cincinnati, OH 45202
Landmark hotel

CITY CLUB
(415) 362-2480
155 Sansome St.
San Francisco, CA 94104
Historic club. Diego Rivera artwork

THE CLEVELAND
RITZ-CARLTON
(216) 623-1300
1515 W. 3rd St.
Cleveland, OH 44113

DALLAS ARBORETUM
& BOTANICAL GARDEN
(214) 327-8263
8525 Garland Rd.
Dallas, TX 75218

DEER VALLEY
(801) 649-1000
P.O. Box 889
Park City, UT 84060

DELANO HOTEL
(800) 555-5001
1685 Collins Ave.
Miami Beach, FL 33139
Full-service planning

DEMENIL RESTAURANT
(314) 771-5829
3352 Demenil Place
St. Louis, MO 63118
**Historic mansion and carriage
house**

THE DUNHILL HOTEL
(800) 354-4141
(704) 332-4141
237 N. Tryon St.
Charlotte, NC 28202

DUNSMUIR HOUSE
AND GARDENS
(510) 562-0328
2960 Peralta Oaks Court
Oakland, CA 94605
**Neoclassical house; 40 acres of
valley meadows and gardens**

ELIZABETH PARK
(860) 722-6490
Hartford, CT
**Historic municipal park, walled
secret garden**

EVERMAY ON-THE-
DELAWARE
(610) 294-9100
P.O. Box 60
Erwinna, PA 18920
Victorian inn with gardens

THE FAIRMONT
HOTEL
(415) 772-5293
950 Mason St.
San Francisco, CA 94108
Ballroom with views

FAIRWINDS ESTATE
(530) 546-3555
P.O. Box 1503
Crystal Bay, NV 89402
Overlooking Lake Tahoe

Banning Residence Museum

THE FEARRINGTON
HOUSE
(919) 542-2121
2000 Fearrington Village Center
Fearrington Village, NC 27312
Formal gardens

THE FOGG MUSEUM
AT HARVARD
(617) 495-0350
32 Quincy St.
Cambridge, MA 02138
Italian Palazzo museum

THE GAMBLE
MANSION
(617) 267-4430 ext. 707
5 Commonwealth Ave.
Boston, MA 02116

GARDENCOURT
(502) 895-3411
c/o Louisville Seminary
1044 Alta Vista Rd.
Louisville, KY 4020,
**19th-century estate, formal
gardens**

THE GEORGIAN SUITE
(212) 734-1468
3 E. 77th St.
New York, NY 10021

THE GEORGIAN
TERRACE
(404) 897-1991
659 Peachtree St.
Atlanta, GA 30308

GILLESPIE COUNTY
HISTORICAL SOCIETY
(830) 997-2835
312 W. San Antonio St.
Fredericksburg, TX 78624
Pioneer museum

GREYSTONE MANSION
(310) 550-4654
905 Loma Vista Dr.
Beverly Hills, CA 90210

GRANT-HUMPHREYS
MANSION
(303) 894-2506
770 Pennsylvania St.
Denver, CO 80203
Historic home; mountain view

HAMLIN MANSION
(415) 331-0544
2120 Broadway
San Francisco, CA 94115

HARBOR VIEW HOTEL
(508) 627-4333
131 North Water St.
Edgartown, MA 02539

THE HEATHMAN
(503) 241-4100
1001 SW Broadway
Portland, OR 97205
1927 tea court

HERITAGE HOUSE
(707) 937-5885
5200 North Highway 1
Little River, CA 95456
**Farmhouse inn overlooking the
Pacific Ocean**

HORNBLOWER YACHTS
(310) 301-6000
13755 Fiji Way
Marina del Rey, CA 90292
Wedding planning

HOTEL BOULDERADO
(303) 442-4344
2115 E. 13th St.
Boulder, CO 80302
**Victorian-era hotel with original
details**

HOTEL DEL
CORONADO
(619) 435-6611
1500 Orange Ave.
Coronado, CA

THE HOTEL DU PONT
(302) 594-3122
11th & Market St.
Wilmington, DE 19801

HOTEL ST. GERMAIN
(214) 871-2516
2516 Maple Ave.
Dallas, TX 75201
**Victorian mansion with French
antiques**

HYATT REGENCY
SCOTTSDALE AT
GAINEY RANCH
(602) 991-3388
7500 East Doubletree Ranch Rd.
Scottsdale, AZ 85258

II CIELO
(310) 276-9990
9018 Burton Way
Beverly Hills, CA 90211

INDIANA ROOF
BALLROOM
(317) 236-1874
140 W. Washington St.
Indianapolis, IN 46204
1927 Spanish Baroque ballroom

INDIANAPOLIS
MUSEUM OF ART
(317) 923-1331
1200 W. 38th St.
Indianapolis, IN 46208
Formal garden, river views

INN AT CASTLE HILL
(401) 849-3800
590 Ocean Dr.
Newport, RI 02840
**Victorian inn overlooks
Narragansett Bay**

THE INN AT HARVARD
(617) 491-2222
1201 Massachusetts Ave.
Cambridge, MA 02138

INN AT LITTLE
WASHINGTON
(540) 675-3800
P.O. Box 300
Washington, VA 22747
Small rural inn

INN AT PERRY CABIN
(410) 745-2200
308 Watkins La.
St. Michael's, MD 21663
**Chesapeake Bay–front inn and
gardens**

INN AT
WEATHERSFIELD
(802) 263-9217
Route 106
Weathersfield, VT 05151
Colonial inn

THE JAMES BREAKY
MANOR
(313) 584-5570
125 N. Huron
Ypsilanti, MI 48197

JAMES BURDEN
AND OTTO KAHN
MANSIONS
(212) 722-4745
1 East 91st St.
New York, NY
**1905 Italian Renaissance mansion
with French interiors**

THE JOHN RUTLEDGE
HOUSE
(803) 723-7999
116 Broad St.
Charleston, SC 29401
**Historic home with ballroom
and small courtyard**

THE JUNIOR LEAGUE
(713) 622-4191
1811 Briar Oaks Lane
Houston, TX 77027
**Ballroom, tearoom, and
courtyard**

LAKE FOREST
ACADEMY
(847) 234-3210
1500 W. Kennedy Rd.
Lake Forest, IL 60045
**Turn-of-the-century Italian
mansion; formal garden**

LARK CREEK INN
(415) 924-7766
234 Magnolia Ave.
Larkspar, CA 94939
Victorian house

THE LEGION OF
HONOR
(415) 263-0229
100 34th Ave.
San Francisco, CA 94121
**Elegant museum cafe and
sculpture garden**

LOCUST GROVE
(502) 897-9845
561 Blankenbaker Ln.
Louisville, KY 40200 1790
Mansion with extensive grounds

LONGVIEW MANSION
(816) 761-6669
3361 SW Longview Rd.
Lee's Summit, MO 64081
1914 mansion

LYFORD HOUSE
(415) 388-2524
376 Greenwood Beach Rd.
Tiburon, CA 94920
**Victorian house in a bird
sanctuary**

THE LYMAN ESTATE
(781) 893-7232
185 Lyman St.
Waltham, MA 02154
1793 mansion

MALMAISON
(314) 458-0131
P.O. Box 107
St. Albans, MO 63073
**Rustic setting with gardens,
fountain, lawns**

MANHATTAN
PENTHOUSE
(212) 627-8838
80 5th Ave.
New York, NY 10011

MASURY MANSION
(516) 878-6373
End of Old Neck Road off the
Montauk Highway
Center Moriches, NY
Formal Adamesque ballroom

MEADOWOOD RESORT
(707) 963-3646
(800) 458-8080
900 Meadowood Ln.
St. Helena, CA 94574

MEMORIAL HALL
(215) 685-0122
Fairmont Park Properties
P.O. Box 21601
Philadelphia, PA 19131
**1876 Great Hall ballroom with
marble floors**

MERIDIAN HOUSE
(202) 667-6670
1630 Crescent Place NW
Washington, DC 20009
**16th-century French townhouse
with gardens**

THE MINT MUSEUM
(704) 337-2000
2730 Randolph Rd.
Charlotte, NC 28207
**Two locations available for
evening receptions**

MISSION INN
(909) 784-0300
3649 Mission Inn Ave.
Riverside, CA 92501
Chapels available

MISSOURI BOTANICAL
GARDEN
(314) 577-5100
4344 Shaw Blvd.
St. Louis, MO 63110

NAPA VALLEY WINE
TRAIN
(707) 253-2111
(800) 427-4124
1275 McKinstry St.
Napa, CA 94559
Weddings held on train

NOERENBERG
GARDENS
(612) 559-6700
2840 North Shore Dr.
Wayzata, MN 55391
**Small formal flower gardens
with gazebo**

OATLANDS
PLANTATION
(703) 777-3174
Rte. 2, Box 352
Leesburg, VA 22075
**Greek Revival mansion
and gardens**

Boulders Inn

SITES

PARK HYATT
PHILADELPHIA
(800) 233-1234
(215) 893-1776
1415 Chancellor Ct.
Philadelphia, PA 19102
Ballroom and rose garden

THE PEABODY HOTEL
(901) 529-4000
149 Union Ave.
Memphis, TN 38103

PHIPPS
CONSERVATORY
(412) 622-6915
1 Shendley Park
Pittsburgh, PA 15213
Gardens with tents

PHIPPS MANSION
(303) 777-4441
3400 Belcaro Dr.
Denver, CO 80209
**Georgian mansion, groomed
lawns, and gardens**

THE PHOENICIAN
(602) 941-8200
6000 E. Camelback Rd.
Scottsdale, AZ 85251
Ballroom and outdoor spaces

PITTSBURGH CENTER
FOR THE ARTS
(412) 361-0873
6300 5th Ave.
Pittsburgh, PA 15212
Gallery and patio

PITTSBURGH'S GRAND
HALL AT THE PRIORY
(412) 231-3338
614 Pressley St.
Pittsburgh, PA 15212
Former Catholic church

PLACES
(212) 737-7536
Box 810 Gracie Sta.
New York, NY 10028
Reception location service

THE POINT
(800) 255-3530
(518) 891-5674
HCR #1 Box 65
Saranac Lake, NY 12983
Great camp with log cabins

THE POLO FIELDS
COUNTRY CLUB
(313) 998-3456
5200 Polo Fields Dr.
Ann Arbor, MI 48103
Ballroom

PORTOBELLO HOTEL
(011) 44-171-727-2777
22 Stanley Gardens
London W11 ZNG
England

POWELL GARDENS
(816) 697-2600 ext. 240
1609 NW U.S. Highway 50
Kingsville, MO 64061
**Botanical gardens and landmark
chapel**

POWELL SYMPHONY
HALL
(314) 533-2500
718 N. Grand Blvd.
St. Louis, MO 63103
Palace of Versailles–style lobby

THE PRATT MANSIONS
(212) 744-4486 ext. 150
1027 Fifth Ave.
New York, NY
**Ballroom with view of the
Metropolitan Museum of Art**

PROSPECT HILL
(800) 277-0844
2887 Poindexter Rd.
Trevilians, VA 23093
1700's style plantation

THE PUCK BUILDING
(212) 274-8900
295 Lafayette St.
New York, NY 10012
Skylit loft; grand ballroom

RALPH SCHNELL
HOUSE
(317) 925-4600
3050 N. Meridian St.
Indianapolis, IN 56208
**1904 Victorian house with
ballroom**

EL RANCHO DE LAS
GOLONDRINAS
(505) 471-2261
334 Los Pinos Rd.
Santa Fe, NM 87505
Hispanic village with chapels

THE RANDALL DAVEY
AUDUBON CENTER
(505) 983-4609
P.O. Box 9314
Santa Fe, NM 87504
**1847 sawmill with formal garden
and orchard**

RED BUTTLE GARDEN
AND ARBORETUM
(801) 585-5225
18A de Trobriand St.
Salt Lake City, UT 84113
**Courtyard with fountain and
flowers; other streamside sites**

RED HILL VINEYARD
(503) 538-0666
30835 North Hwy. 99W
Newberg, OR 97132
Tasting room and gardens

RIPPAVILLA
(615) 496-9037
5700 Main St.
Spring Hill, TN 37174
Antebellum estate

RITTENHOUSE HOTEL
(800) 635-1042
(215) 546-9000
210 W. Rittenhouse Square
Philadelphia, PA 19103
Ballroom

Masury Mansion

RIVER OAKS GARDEN
CLUB
(713) 523-2483
2503 Westheimer Rd.
Houston, TX 77098
Banquet hall and gardens

THE RUINS
(206) 285-7846
570 Roy St.
Seattle, WA 98109
Gardens, courtyards

SADDLE PEAK LODGE
(818) 222-3888
419 Cold Canyon Rd.
Calabasas, CA 91302
Lodge with mountain views

ST. ALBANS STUDIO
(314) 458-5356
P.O.Box 49
173 St. Albans Rd.
St. Albans, MO 63073
1920's style reception site; hunting lodge available

ST. LOUIS ART
MUSEUM
(314) 721-0072
Forest Park #1, Fine Arts Dr.
St. Louis, MO 63110
Sculpture terrace with waterwall

SEVEN GABLES INN
(314) 863-8400
26 N. Meramec
Clayton, MO 63105
Garden court and formal dining room

SHUTTERS ON THE
BEACH
(310) 458-0030
1 Pico Blvd.
Santa Monica, CA 90405

THE STANHOPE
HOTEL
(212) 288-5800
995 Fifth Ave.
New York, NY 10028

STEMSON GREEN
MANSION
(206) 624-0474
1204 Minor St.
Seattle, WA 98101
Turn-of-the-century mansion

STERN GROVE
TROCADERO CLUB
HOUSE
(415) 831-5500
19th Ave. and Sloat Blvd.
San Francisco, CA 94116

STONE MANOR
(310) 457-6285
Malibu, CA
Ocean-view estate, formal gardens

STOW ACRES
COUNTRY CLUB
(978) 568-8106
58 Randall Rd.
Stow, MA 01775
Victorian room

STRATHMORE ART
CENTER
(301) 530-5889
10701 Rockville Pike
N. Bethesda, MD 20852
Large estate

SWEDENBORGIAN
CHURCH
(415) 346-6466
2107 Lyon St.(location)
San Francisco, CA 94115
1895 Arts and Crafts building

TEGA CAY GOLF CLUB
(803) 548-3500
1 Molokai Dr.
P.O. Drawer 39
Tega Cay, SC 29715

THISTLE HILL
(817) 336-1212
1509 Pennsylvania Ave.
Fort Worth, TX 76104

UNA ESTATE-
SOYUZIVKA
(914) 626-5641
Foordmore Rd.
Kerhonkson, NY

UNION STATION
(213) 830-6687
800 N. Alameda St.
Los Angeles, CA 90012
Former California Mission-style train station

Oatlands Plantation

UNION STATION
HOTEL
(615) 726-1001
1001 Broadway
Nashville, TN 37203

VILLA MONTALVO
(408) 961-5814
15400 Montalvo Rd.
Saratoga, CA 95071

WAVE HILL
(718) 549-3200
675 West 252nd St.
Bronx, NY 10011
Historic estate with river view and gardens

WHEATLEIGH
(413) 637-0610
P.O. Box 824 and Hawthorne Rd.
Lenox, MA, 01240
1893 Italian palazzo-style hotel

WILLOW RIDGE
(303) 697-6951
4903 Willow Springs Rd.
Morrison, CO 80465
18th-century mansion with ballroom

WEDDING
HISTORIAN

STEWART, ARLENE
HAMILTON
(914) 232-8973
Katonah, NY 10536
By appointment